WORLD OF SHAKESPEARE
ANIMALS AND MONSTERS

WORLD OF SHAKESPEARE

*

PLANTS
ANIMALS AND MONSTERS
SPORTS AND PASTIMES
TECHNOLOGY
MAGIC AND SUPERSTITION

WORLD OF SHAKESPEARE:
ANIMALS & MONSTERS

ALAN DENT

WITH A FOREWORD BY

SIR RALPH RICHARDSON

TAPLINGER PUBLISHING COMPANY
NEW YORK

First published in the United States in 1973 by
TAPLINGER PUBLISHING CO., INC.
New York, New York

Copyright © 1972 by Alan Dent
All rights reserved.
Printed in Great Britain

Library of Congress Catalog Card Number: 72-13625
ISBN 0-8008-0274-8

FOREWORD

Prepare now for another trip round the World of Shakespeare with Alan Dent. This is a quick-witted critic who is always on the move, and it was only last year that he took us botanizing with *World of Shakespeare: Plants*. This was an exhilarating and surprising excursion and some memorable pressings were collected. Now we will go a-hunting for animals and monsters.

I think everyone who knows Alan Dent will agree that there is an additional pleasure to be gained from these little books in that they are very *like* him – they catch his character so vividly. I imagine that everyone, in world of theatre, of music, and of books, does know Alan Dent. But just to make sure – in case there might remain some unhappy few who are not yet acquainted with him – I will take a snapshot.

He was cut in Scottish granite in Ayrshire early in this century. One might have expected that such a figure would have remained there among the heather and the thistles all his life. But, at an early age, Alan Dent was struck by a cataleptic seizure – he was, in fact, stage-struck, and this so severely that it sent him hurtling to London where he apprenticed himself to the great dramatic critic, James Agate. It was during that time, in the late 'twenties, that I first met him. Then we were both rather young, though he was a little younger than I was. He has changed little in manner or appearance in all those years. His hair has, indeed, gone rather grey. But there he is lucky, for mine has just gone.

His manner has always been courteous and grave. The casual or couldn't-care-less air is unknown to him; one feels that he has just come from some important ceremony, perhaps at the College of Heralds. He is very companionable and easy to talk to, modest and unassertive, but not so reticent about himself that he will fail to draw responsive confidence from a friend.

His memory is astonishing, and he decorates his conversation – as he has so profusely illustrated his books – with glimpses into his rich supply of theatre lore and literary and musical reminiscence.

Until last week I should have called him a very observant man, for how else could he have stored his memory so surprisingly? But last week he quite failed to notice me across the Haymarket! I espied him at a little distance: he was striding out, of course – no Regency dawdle about *him*. I waved – I smiled – I lobbed a 'Hello, Alan,' across. He never blinked, but instantly vanished under Nash's graceful and classic portico and into the theatre, as if he'd found a bolt-hole. But perhaps he had indeed observed me, and thought he'd seen a monster, Shakespearean or otherwise?

Alan is a pedantical man, in the least dry and most pedantical sense of the word. And I think that his declared hobby will illustrate this, and can conclude my snapshot. In *Who's Who in the Theatre* he declares his hobby to be SERENDIPITY. This is, of course, as everyone knows – and I know too, when I had sent out for a dictionary – 'always making discoveries, by accident and sagacity, of things one is not in search of'.

RALPH RICHARDSON

CONTENTS

Contents

AGENTS AND FAMILIARS

It is, very justly, through the mouth of Macbeth that Shakespeare deploys his most sinister use of a casual-seeming word like 'agent' to connote all the powers of evil; and it is done in two lines in the speech Macbeth makes after completing his plan for the murder of Banquo (III, ii, 51):

> Good things of day begin to droop and drowse,
> Whiles night's black **agents** to their preys do rouse.

A Familiar, also in its more sinister sense and used as a noun, was the companion or common attendant of a witch, and usually an evil spirit disguised as a cat, dog or other animal. La Pucelle, Shakespeare's version of Joan of Arc in *King Henry VI, Part One*, is little better than a witch, though a very courageous one; and Talbot asks the Duke of Burgundy about her and mentions her usual companion without specifying its nature (III, ii, 121):

> Thanks, gentle Duke. But where is Pucelle now?
> I think her old **familiar** is asleep.

In a later scene in the same play La Pucelle uses the same word, though adjectivally, to a group of Fiends (not Angels) whom she conjures up in a clap of thunder, appealing to them for help which they refuse (v, iii, 8):

> This speedy and quick appearance **argues** proof
> Of your accustom'd diligence **to** me.
> Now, ye **familiar** spirits that are cull'd
> Out of the powerful legions under earth,
> Help me this once, that France may get the field.
> O, hold me not with silence over-long!
> Where I was wont to feed you with my blood, . . .

But the Fiends 'walk, and speak not, and hang their heads';
and then vanish without helping. It is all very *fürchtenmachend*,
as Germans would say – chilling rather than warming.

ALLIGATOR AND CROCODILE

The Alligator is agreeably called 'an allegory on the banks of
the Nile' by Sheridan's Mrs Malaprop. But the *Oxford English
Dictionary* calls it, much less agreeably, 'a genus of Saurians of
the crocodile family', and goes on to say that in popular usage
alligators are 'all large American Saurians, some of which are
true crocodiles'. With relief one turns from the biological
muddle to Shakespeare's world. And there we find that the
alligator exists only as a stuffed corpse in the apothecary's shop
to which Romeo goes to purchase poison (*Romeo and Juliet*, v,
i, 37):

> I do remember an apothecary,
> And hereabouts he dwells, which late I noted . . .
> And in his needy shop a tortoise hung,
> An **alligator** stuff'd, and other skins
> Of ill-shap'd fishes; . . .

Away back in 1935 the needy apothecary in this little scene
was vividly played by a new young actor called Alec Guinness;
and this commentator concluded his very first review in the
Manchester Guardian (as it then was) with the query and the
comment: 'Why does Shakespeare make him fuss so much at
being paid by Romeo? Perhaps in Mantua the chemists were
not cash?'

The Crocodile itself has familiar mention in *Hamlet*,
Othello and *Antony and Cleopatra*. But one would rather note
the unfamiliar passage in which Queen Margaret says the

King must be wary of Gloster (*King Henry VI, Part Two*, III, i, 224):

> Henry, my lord, is cold in great affairs,
> Too full of foolish pity; and Gloster's show
> Beguiles him as the mournful **crocodile**
> With sorrow snares relenting passengers; . . .

The reference is to the hideous old legend that when a crocodile swallowed a man it could leave his head unswallowed out of pity, hence the phrase 'crocodile tears'. One would rather think the monster leaves it uneaten out of distaste, as a thing unpalatable, very much as a man repudiates the head of a fish or a rabbit or a chicken.

ANCHOVIES AND HERRINGS

These are bracketed together because both belong to the same fishy family. Anchovies occur only in Falstaff's bill for supper at the end of the great Eastcheap Tavern scene in the heart of *King Henry IV, Part One* (II, iv, 520):

> Item, **anchovies** and sack after supper . . . *2s. 6d.*

Herrings occur much oftener, but usually only in metaphor. Feste, describing his position in the Lady Olivia's household, says to Viola, 'I am indeed not her fool, but her corrupter of words', and says also, 'She will keep no fool, sir, till she be married; and fools are as like husbands as pilchers are to **herrings** – the husband's the bigger.' (*Twelfth Night*, III, i, 31). In the same play (I, v, 114) the same fish cause Sir Toby's one and only belch, 'A plague o' these pickle-**herring** !'

[11]

ANIMALS IN GENERAL

In perhaps the loftiest of all his prose speeches Hamlet rates
mankind as 'the beauty of the world! the paragon of **animals**!'
(*Hamlet*, II, ii, 306) only to go on characteristically, 'And yet,
to me, what is this quintessence of dust?'

Jaques, in *As You Like It*, has a humane dislike of hunting as
a sport, and is described to the Banished Duke as 'commenting
upon the sobbing deer' and as inveighing against the practice
of hunting throughout the land (II, i, 58):

> Thus most invectively he pierceth through
> The body of the country, city, court,
> Yea, and of this our life; swearing that we
> Are mere usurpers, tyrants, and what's worse,
> To fright the **animals**, and to kill them up
> In their assign'd and native dwelling-place.

A little earlier in the same speech Jaques is described as
'weeping into the needless stream'. The adjective is so printed
in the First Folio (when the play first appeared) and 'needless'
appears with slavish conformity in every subsequent edition
one has ever seen. Yet surely 'heedless' makes far better sense.
Can this be an example of what may be called 'perpetual
misprint'?

The synonymous and slightly more pejorative word 'beasts'
occurs even more frequently – nowhere perhaps more strikingly than in Prospero's threat to punish his reluctant slave,
Caliban (*The Tempest*, I, ii, 366):

> Hag-seed, hence!
> Fetch us in fuel. And be quick, thou'rt best,
> To answer other business. Shrug'st thou, malice?
> If thou neglect'st, or dost unwillingly

What I command, I'll rack thee with old cramps,
Fill all thy bones with aches, make thee roar,
That **beasts** shall tremble at thy din.

In *The Comedy of Errors* (II, i, 15) Luciana, who is the spinster sister of Mrs Antipholus of Ephesus, has a by-no-means uninteresting homily on the subject of marriage:

Why, headstrong liberty is lash'd with woe.
There's nothing situate under heaven's eye
But hath his bound, in earth, in sea, in sky.
The **beasts**, the fishes, and the winged fowls,
Are their males' subjects, and at their controls.
Man more divine, the master of all these,
Lord of the wide world and wild wat'ry seas,
Indu'd with intellectual sense and souls,
Of more pre-eminence than fish and fowls,
Are masters to their females, and their lords;
Then let your will attend on their accords.

To which the married Adriana has the tart reply of a single line – 'This servitude makes you to keep unwed.'

ASPS, ADDERS, VIPERS

The Asp, oddly enough, is not mentioned by that name in the text of *Antony and Cleopatra*. It is three times given its old poetic form of 'aspic' in the last act. 'Have I the **aspic** in my lips?' (V, ii, 291) says Cleopatra when her maid Iras falls dead. And after Cleopatra's own death her guardsman attendant, taking up the fig basket, has a line of explanation of which – Heaven knows why! – he is usually deprived (V, ii, 358):

This is an **aspic's** trail, and these fig-leaves
Have slime upon them, such as th' **aspic** leaves
Upon the caves of Nile.

On several other occasions in the same place – it is the culmination of what is surely the greatest of great plays – the creature is insistently referred to as the 'worm' by both Cleopatra and the Clown who brings it. Thus Cleopatra says to this 'rural fellow' who bring her figs (v, ii, 141):

> Hast thou the pretty **worm** of Nilus there
> That kills and pains not?

The bearer says to her, 'I wish you all joy of the worm.' Cleopatra addresses the same slayer as 'thou mortal wretch' and 'poor venomous fool', and then – most thrillingly and movingly – refers to it as her 'baby' in her death speech addressed to Charmian:

> Peace, peace!
> Dost thou not see my baby at my breast
> That sucks the nurse asleep?

The Asp appears too – though again in the form of 'aspic' – in one of Othello's direst eruptions of jealous rage, spoken in Iago's presence (*Othello*, III, iii, 444):

> Arise, black vengeance, from thy hollow cell.
> Yield up, O love, thy crown and hearted throne
> To tyrannous hate! Swell, bosom, with thy fraught,
> For 'tis of **aspics'** tongues.

The Aspic, as Shakespeare calls it, is principally from 'the caves of Nile'. It is a small, venomous, hooded serpent and it is still found in Egypt and Libya.

The Adder or Viper – pretty much the same thing, the non-herpetologist imagines – sidles often and often into the plays, and then slithers out again after no more than a line or two.

'**Adder's** fork and blind-worm's sting' are among the ingredients of the hell-broth prepared by the Witches in their cauldron in *Macbeth* (IV, i, 16). Timon of Athens, that noble misanthrope and highly articulate ass, finds in the play of the same name (IV, iii, 180) that the earth, while he is digging it,

> Engenders the black toad and **adder** blue,
> The gilded newt and eyeless venom'd worm,
> With all th' abhorred births below crisp heaven,
> Whereon Hyperion's quick'ning fire doth shine.

And there are several other reptilian glimpses in the plays.

There are references also, less familiar but no less striking, in the poems. Thus Venus in a myrtle grove is alarmed by the baying of dogs which suggests that her Adonis is engaged on a boar-hunt (lines 877–882):

> By this, she hears the hounds are at a bay;
> Whereat she starts, like one that spies an **adder**
> Wreath'd up in fatal folds just in his way,
> The fear whereof doth make him shake and shudder; . . .

And Lucrece, soliloquizing in her distress, has a meditation on the theme that 'no perfection is so absolute That some impurity doth not pollute', and phrases it thus (lines 869–872):

> Unruly blasts wait on the tender spring;
> Unwholesome weeds take root with precious flow'rs;
> The **adder** hisses where the sweet birds sing;
> What virtue breeds iniquity devours. . . .

The word 'viper' itself is usually in Shakespeare a mere term of abuse, as when Pistol in his vilification of Corporal Nym says, 'O **viper** vile!' in *King Henry V* (II, i, 44). But the adjectival form of the same word, qualifying 'worm' for double emphasis, is used by Henry VI in his derogation of civil war (*King Henry VI, Part One*, III, i, 72):

> Civil dissension is a **viperous** worm
> That gnaws the bowels of the commonwealth.

ASSES

'What are we, Apemantus? says Timon (*Timon of Athens*, II, ii, 64), and Apemantus gives him the answer 'Asses'. He uses the word figuratively, as is usual throughout the plays, to signify something no better than a fool.

We may pick out a phrase fitting Troilus from the bitter railing of Thersites (*Troilus and Cressida*, V, iv, 5): 'That same young Trojan **ass**, that loves the whore there'. And the jealous Mr Ford has twelve loaded words about the un-jealous Mr Page in *The Merry Wives of Windsor* (II, ii, 301): 'Page is an **ass**, a secure **ass**: he will trust his wife; . . .', which flashlights the characters of both these husbands. Dogberry too repeatedly insists on being 'writ down an **ass**' in *Much Ado About Nothing* (IV, ii, 73).

Much of the fun of Bully Bottom lies in the fact that, when he is 'translated' from man to beast, he keeps calling himself an ass without realizing that he has temporarily become one, not only in his head but in his appetites. Thus Puck, in his longish speech to Oberon who wants to know what has been happening in 'this haunted grove' (*A Midsummer Night's Dream*, III, ii, 5), begins his explanation: 'My mistress with a monster is in love,' and concludes:

> I led them on in this distracted fear,
> And left sweet Pyramus translated there;
> When in that moment, so it came to pass,
> Titania wak'd, and straightway lov'd an **ass**.

The most controversial ass of all is Hamlet's when (II, ii, 388) the Strolling Players are at hand and the Prince has this very odd little colloquy with Polonius:

> POLONIUS: The actors are come hither, my lord.
> HAMLET: Buz, buz!

POLONIUS: Upon my honour –
HAMLET: Then came each actor on his **ass** –
POLONIUS: The best actors in the world, etc.

This may be interpreted in a variety of ways. The very latest thing in Hamlets – young Ian McKellen – makes a mad buzzing of bees out of his first comment, and out of his second distinctly and plainly says, 'Then came each actor on his arse', clearly meaning the human fundament or backside. This is underlined by the players making their entry as tumblers, one after the other, as has often been done before. The present age is so permissive that no criticism of this well-travelled production drew any particular attention to this reading.

The only editor of old who spent any ingenuity on the episode is Hudson: 'Hamlet affects to discredit the news: all a mere buzzing or rumour. Polonius then assures him, "On my honour"; which starts the poor joke, "If they are come on your honour, 'then came each actor on his *ass*'"; (so punctuated) these latter words being probably a quotation from some ballad.'

All this is laboured, and surely disingenuous rather than ingenious. Quotes within quotes within quotes!

BABOONS, APES, MARMOSETS

The simians (or *Simiadae*) are almost as frequent as the snakes and reptiles. The oddest of the references to Apes is in that oddest of all the plays, *Love's Labour's Lost* (III, i, 89), where Moth says:

> The fox, the **ape**, and the humble-bee,
> Were still at odds, being but three.
> Until the goose came out of door,
> Staying the odds by adding four.

This is twice repeated, between Moth and Don Adriano de Armado, his master. M. R. Ridley in the New Temple Shakespeare has this note: 'The emphasis laid by repetition on this doggerel indicates clearly enough that it had some piquant topical flavour which, for us, it has wholly lost.' But why 'clearly enough'?

Apemantus in *Timon of Athens* sneers at the time-serving guests who cluster round Timon who is still at the peak of his prosperity (I, i, 251):

> That there should be small love 'mongst these sweet knaves,
> And all this courtesy! The strain of man's bred out
> Into **baboon** and monkey.

The Baboon likewise proves as useful as arrowroot to the Witches in their cooking of hell-broth (*Macbeth*, IV, i, 37):

> Cool it with a **baboon's** blood,
> Then the charm is firm and good.

And the same word is used by Falstaff as a mere term of abuse in *King Henry IV, Part Two* (II, iv, 229):

> DOLL: They say Poins has a good wit.
> FALSTAFF: He a good wit! hang him, **baboon**!
> His wit's as thick as Tewksbury mustard; . . .

A smaller sort of Monkey was one of the wild things of Prospero's island which Caliban proposed to find for his new master Trinculo in *The Tempest* (II, ii, 157):

> I prithee let me bring thee where crabs grow;
> And I with my long nails will dig thee pig-nuts;
> Show thee a jay's nest, and instruct thee how
> To snare the nimble **marmoset**; . . .

Oberon envisages what may happen to his queen Titania after the love-philtre is applied to her sleeping eyes (*M.N.D.*, II, i, 179):

[18]

The next thing then she waking looks upon,
Be it on lion, bear, or wolf, or bull,
On meddling **monkey**, or on busy **ape**,
She shall pursue it with the soul of love.

Instead of which she falls in love with an Athenian weaver wearing an ass's head (temporarily).

Falstaff, soliloquizing in prose, recalls Justice Shallow in the old days (*King Henry IV, Part Two*, III, ii, 324) when he was 'lecherous as a **monkey**, and the whores call'd him mandrake'. And Othello, even while welcoming Lodovico to Cyprus, lets fall his terrible phrase in condemnation of disloyalty (IV, i, 262): 'Goats and **monkeys**!' like a splash of boiling water. Vividly one recollects Laurence Olivier here.

BASILISK AND COCKATRICE

By definition the Basilisk is a fabulous monster 'hatched by a serpent from a cock's egg' – though the ability of a cock to lay an egg is a circumstance beyond my ken. Its breath and even its look was said to be fatal. In *King Henry V* (V, ii, 17) the Queen of France has a difficult line in her speech to the King of England, when she tells him how glad she is to see him smiling at last and no longer glaring with 'the fatal balls of murdering **basilisks**'.

Gloster, in the middle of *King Henry VI, Part Three*, has a long soliloquy so much in the vein of the opening of *King Richard III* that Olivier interpolated much of it into the opening soliloquy of his own film version of the latter play. (Years earlier the American actor, John Barrymore, made a gramophone recording of this speech from the older play which is still well worth hearing. It begins, 'Ay, Edward will use women honourably!')

The same intensely Glosterian speech has the lines (III, ii, 182):

> Why, I can smile, and murder whiles I smile;
> And cry 'Content' to that which grieves my heart;
> And wet my cheeks with artificial tears,
> And frame my face to all occasions:
> I'll drown more sailors than the mermaid shall;
> I'll slay more gazers than the **basilisk**; . . .

In *King Richard III*, again, Gloster has a pretty exchange with the Lady Anne, who has just spat upon him (I, ii, 144):

GLOSTER: Why dost thou spit at me?
LADY ANNE: Would it were mortal poison, for thy sake!
GLOSTER: Never came poison from so sweet a place.
LADY ANNE: Never hung poison on a fouler toad.
    Out of my sight! thou dost infect mine eyes.
GLOSTER: Thine eyes, sweet lady, have infected mine.
LADY ANNE: Would they were **basilisks**, to strike thee dead!

It must be guessed that 'Cockatrice' is another name for the same dubious and deadly monster. Sir Toby Belch in *Twelfth Night* tells us of the device whereby he makes both Viola and Sir Andrew too scared to engage one another in a duel (III, iv, 185): 'This will so fright them both, that they will kill one another by the look, like **cockatrices**.' Juliet says of the cockatrice that it has a 'death-darting eye' (*Romeo and Juliet*, III, ii, 47). The old Duchess of York in *King Richard III* says of the same horror that its 'unavoided eye is murderous' (IV, i, 55). And the ravisher of Lucrece has 'a **cockatrice**' dead-killing eye' (*The Rape of Lucrece*, 540).

BATS AND LEECHES

These be blood-suckers. 'Wool of **bat** and tongue of dog' are among the dire things that boil and bubble in the Witches' cauldron (*Macbeth*, IV, i, 15); and Macbeth himself, telling his lady that Banquo and Fleance still live and breathe, has a speech that is among the most cold-blooded in the whole play (III, ii, 39):

> There's comfort yet; they are assailable;
> Then be thou jocund: ere the **bat** hath flown
> His cloister'd flight . . . there shall be done
> A deed of dreadful note.

In *The Tempest* Caliban curses Prospero with 'all the charms of Sycorax, toads, beetles, **bats**' (I, ii, 339). But to Ariel in the most aerial of his songs the bat is merely a flying machine (v, i, 91):

> On the **bat's** back I do fly
> After summer merrily.

It is somewhat odd that the incubus, the succubus, and the vampire bat, all occurring in Elizabethan and earlier literature, are nowhere mentioned by Shakespeare. The only mention of the leech is figurative and is to be found at the very end of *Timon of Athens*. Alcibiades, advancing to self-promotion in Athens, utters these, the very last, lines in the play (v, iv, 79):

> Dead
> Is noble Timon: of whose memory
> Hereafter more. Bring me into your city,
> And I will use the olive with my sword:
> Make war breed peace; make peace stint war; make each
> Prescribe to other, as each other's **leech**.
> Let our drums strike.
>
> [*Exeunt*

There is also Pistol's resonant line or two in *King Henry V* (ii, iii, 56):

> Yoke-fellows in arms,
> Let us to France, like **horse-leeches**, my boys,
> To suck, to suck, the very blood to suck!

This wrings a remark from the Boy who is not bloody-minded, 'And that's but unwholesome food, they say.'

BEARS

The Bear to Shakespeare was a familiar creature, and he usually writes vividly and imaginatively about it. Thus Prospero tells Ariel of the torments from which his master released him (*The Tempest*, I, ii, 287):

> ... thy groans
> Did make wolves howl, and penetrate the breasts
> Of ever-angry **bears**: ...

Falstaff describes himself to Prince Hal as being 'as melancholy as a gib-cat or a lugg'd [i.e. baited] **bear**' (*King Henry IV, Part One*, I, ii, 72). The Duke of Orleans describes English mastiffs as 'foolish curs, that run winking into the mouth of a Russian **bear**, and have their heads crusht like rotten apples' (*King Henry V*, III, vii, 137). Ajax is thus described to Cressida, 'He is as valiant as the lion, churlish as the **bear**, slow as the elephant' (*Troilus and Cressida*, I, ii, 20). 'Chain me with roaring **bears**,' says Juliet to Friar Laurence as an alternative to being married to Paris (*Romeo and Juliet*, IV, i, 80). Decius Brutus (in *Julius Caesar*, II, i, 203) tells us how Caesar

> loves to hear
> That unicorns may be betray'd with trees,
> And **bears** with glasses, ...

Macbeth says fearfully to the Ghost of Banquo (*Macbeth*, III, iv, 100):

> Approach thou like the rugged Russian **bear**,
> The arm'd rhinoceros, or the Hyrcan tiger;
> Take any shape but that, . . .

Lear describes himself to his daughter Goneril (*King Lear*, IV, ii, 41) as

> A father, and a gracious aged man,
> Whose reverence even the head-lugg'd **bear** would lick, . . .

Othello calls his wife 'an admirable musician! O, she will sing the savageness out of a **bear**!' (*Othello*, IV, i, 185).

All these things, and many other such, are high images suggested by the bear. But we may sense the bear itself, the actual animal harried and worried and teased by dogs to make an Elizabethan holiday, in the poet's only comedy of the workaday life around him as he wrote.

All this is contained in a snatch of conversation in *The Merry Wives of Windsor* between Slender and Anne Page (I, i, 262), a snatch which is rich in actual information as well as in grounds for surmise:

SLENDER: Why do your dogs bark so? Be there **bears** i' th' town?
ANNE: I think there are, sir; I heard them talk'd of.
SLENDER: I love the sport well; but I shall as soon quarrel at it as any man in England. You are afraid, if you see the **bear** loose, are you not?
ANNE: Ay, indeed, sir.
SLENDER: That's meat and drink to me, now. I have seen Sackerson loose twenty times, and have taken him by the chain; but, I warrant you, the women have so cried and shriek'd at it, that it pass'd; but women, indeed, cannot abide 'em; they are very ill-favour'd rough things.

BEETLES AND BUGS

There is something diabolical about the Beetle, whether in Shakespeare or out of it. Not for nothing is it one of the familiars of witches, like the bat, the toad, and the owl. In this direct sense it is mentioned in *The Tempest* as one of the associates of the foul witch who was Caliban's mother. Thus Caliban snarls against Prospero (I, ii, 339):

> All the charms
> Of Sycorax, toads, **beetles**, bats, light on you!

In *Measure for Measure* it is the subject of a metaphysical aphorism, made by Isabella, which might be defined as more emotional than intellectual (III, i, 75):

> The sense of death is most in apprehension;
> And the poor **beetle** that we tread upon,
> In corporal sufferance finds a pang as great
> As when a giant dies.

But in the three really sinister mentions of this coleopterate creature it is always 'shard-borne', and neither the English dictionaries nor the Shakespearean scholars can tell us what this adjective means. Does it mean 'born out of dung' like the so-called dung beetle or dor (*Geotrupes Stercorarius*), which is declared by the *Oxford English Dictionary* to fly after sunset? Or does it mean 'carried along by shards', which are scaly cases that conceal the wings proper?

Jean-Henri Fabre, the Belgian entomologist, said in his *The Glow-Worm and Other Beetles* that *Stercorarius*, 'black in all parts exposed to the light of day, displays a ventral surface of a glorious amethyst violet'. This aged scientist studied beetles so closely and for so many years that he ended up looking rather like one.

In *Antony and Cleopatra* we have Agrippa and Enobarbus discussing Lepidus and his affection for Octavius and Antony (III, ii, 19):

> AGRIPPA: Both he loves.
> ENOBARBUS: They are his shards, and he their **beetle**.

In *Cymbeline* old Belisarius says to his two boys (III, iii, 19):

> . . . often, to our comfort, shall we find
> The sharded **beetle** in a safer hold
> Than is the full-wing'd eagle.

And Macbeth, much more familiarly, hints darkly to his wife concerning the imminent murder of Banquo and his son (*Macbeth*, III, ii, 39):

> Then be thou jocund: ere the bat hath flown
> His cloister'd flight; ere, to black Hecate's summons,
> The shard-borne **beetle** with his drowsy hums
> Hath rung night's yawning peal, there shall be done
> A deed of dreadful note.

Dover Wilson in his Cambridge Shakespeare (1947) at least allows that 'the meaning is disputed in all three instances'. He also quotes Professor Grierson's translation of what it is that the shard-borne beetle has done 'with his drowsy hums'; he 'hath tolled night's slumbrous curfew'. But surely this is professorial non-poetry!

One would rather say that this – like some half-dozen other passages in *Macbeth* – is one of those phrases too highly poetical to be truly meaningful. And one would repeat that the beetle in Shakespeare, whether shard-borne or otherwise, is diabolical.

BIRDS IN GENERAL

These sing, or are silent, throughout the plays and the poems. The references are simply too many to choose amongst. So one concentrates on a single sonnet, and gives four lines of it without any comment whatsoever. It is the opening of Sonnet 73:

> That time of year thou mayst in me behold
> When yellow leaves, or none, or few, do hang
> Upon those boughs which shake against the cold,
> Bare ruin'd choirs, where late the sweet **birds** sang.

BLACKBIRD AND OUSEL

The Blackbird (*Tardus merula*), one of our best-loved songsters with the liquid throat, is referred to very rarely and only by its old name of 'ousel'.

This is used figuratively and as a term of mild disparagement in an interchange in Gloucestershire, early one morning, between Justice Shallow and Justice Silence (*King Henry IV, Part Two*, III, ii, I):

SHALLOW: Come on, come on, come on, sir; give me your hand, sir, give me your hand, sir: an early stirrer, by the rood! And how doth my good cousin Silence?

SILENCE: Good morrow, good cousin Shallow.

SHALLOW: And how doth my good cousin, your bedfellow? and your fairest daughter and mine, my god-daughter Ellen?

SILENCE: Alas, a black **ousel**, cousin Shallow!

We hear, and know, no more about Ellen.

But the bird itself appears vividly in Bottom the Weaver's

little ditty about birds in general (*A Midsummer Night's Dream*, III, i, 124), the song that begins:

> The **ousel**-cock so black of hue,
> With orange-tawny bill, . . .

This, by the way, in the First Folio agreeably appears as follows:

> The Woosell cocke, so blacke of hew,
> With Orenge-tawny bill . . .

As Mark Twain might say, their spelling in those early days left much to be desired. Or as an earlier American, Artemus Ward, said of an earlier poet, 'It is a pity that Chawcer, who had geneyus, was so unedicated. He's the wuss speller I know of.'

BULLS AND OXEN

Theseus in *A Midsummer Night's Dream* is as proud of his hounds as the Dauphin in *Henry V* was of his horse. And he goes so far as to compare them with bulls (IV, i, 120):

> My hounds are bred out of the Spartan kind,
> So flew'd, so sanded; and their heads are hung
> With ears that sweep away the morning dew;
> Crook-knee'd, and dew-lapt like Thessalian **bulls**; . . .

In *The Tempest* it is the sound of savage bulls, or maybe of lions, that wakes the shipwrecked noblemen from their first slumber on Prospero's island. The honest old counsellor, Gonzalo, gets the chance for a laugh from the last word in the passage (II, i, 302):

GONZALO: Now, good angels
Preserve the king!

ALONSO: Why, how now? ho, awake!
. . . wherefore this ghastly looking?
GONZALO: What's the matter?
SEBASTIAN: Whiles we stood here securing your repose,
  Even now, we heard a hollow burst of bellowing
  Like **bulls**, or rather lions: did't not wake you?
  It struck mine ear most terribly.
ALONSO: I heard nothing.
ANTONIO: O, 'twas a din to fright a monster's ear,
  To make an earthquake! sure, it was the roar
  Of a whole herd of lions.
ALONSO: Heard you this, Gonzalo?
GONZALO: Upon mine honour, sir, I heard a humming, . . .

The isle is full of noises and hummings.

BUTTERFLIES

Five times only does a butterfly flutter into the great garden of
Shakespeare's drama, and always with the prettiest and fleetest
effect.

One of them is chased by the unseen little boy who is
Coriolanus' son – unseen but vividly and naturally depicted
by his mother and his wife, Volumnia and Virgilia, and the
visiting lady, Valeria (*Coriolanus,* I, iii, 56):

VALERIA: How does your little son?
VIRGILIA: I thank your ladyship; well, good madam.
VOLUMNIA: He had rather see the swords, and hear a drum, than
  look upon his schoolmaster.
VALERIA: O' my word, the father's son: I'll swear, 'tis a very pretty
  boy. O' my troth, I lookt upon him o' Wednesday half an hour
  together: has such a confirm'd countenance. I saw him run after a
  gilded **butterfly**; and when he caught it, he let it go again; and
  after it again; and over and over he comes, and up again; catcht it

[28]

again: or whether his fall enraged him, or how 'twas, he did so
set his teeth, and tear it: O, I warrant, how he mammockt it!
VOLUMNIA: One on's father's moods.

Later in the same play, Cominius comments on Coriolanus
and his way with the Volscians to his friend Menenius (IV, vi,
91):

> He is their god: he leads them like a thing
> Made by some other deity than nature,
> That shapes man better; and they follow him,
> Against us brats, with no less confidence
> Than boys pursuing summer **butterflies,**
> Or butchers killing flies.

Titania has a charming behest to her attendant-fays that her
sleeping Bottom may not be disturbed (*M.N.D.*, III, i, 171):

> And pluck the wings from painted **butterflies**
> To fan the moonbeams from his sleeping eyes:
> Nod to him, elves, and do him courtesies.

Achilles philosophizes to Patroclus on the way of the world
(*Troilus and Cressida*, III, iii, 75):

> 'Tis certain, greatness, once faln out with fortune,
> Must fall out with men too: what the declined is,
> He shall as soon read in the eyes of others
> As feel in his own fall; for men, like **butterflies,**
> Show not their mealy wings but to the summer; . . .

And the aged Lear, though in captivity, has the comfort of his
youngest daughter, and is too racked and buffeted to care even
for liberty (*King Lear*, v, iii, 7):

CORDELIA: Shall we not see these daughters and these sisters?
LEAR: No, no, no, no! Come, let's away to prison:
  We two alone will sing like birds i' the cage:
  When thou dost ask me blessing, I'll kneel down,

And ask of thee forgiveness: so we'll live,
And pray, and sing, and tell old tales, and laugh
At gilded **butterflies**, and hear poor rogues
Talk of court news; and we'll talk with them too,
Who loses and who wins; who's in, who's out;
And take upon's the mystery of things,
As if we were God's spies: . . .

Of this century's four or five worthy Lears, Gielgud was here the most memorable and the most shattering.

BUZZARDS

If we permit ourselves to say that that ineffectual hawk, the Buzzard, buzzes through only two of the plays, we may also hasten to add that the word-play is not ours but that of the shrew-tamer, Petruchio (*The Taming of the Shrew*, II, i, 199):

KATHARINA: Asses are made to bear, and so are you.
PETRUCHIO: Women are made to bear, and so are you.
KATHARINA: No such jade as you, if me you mean.
PETRUCHIO: Alas, good Kate! I will not burthen thee!
  For, knowing thee to be but young and light –
KATHARINA: Too light for such a swain as you to catch;
  And yet as heavy as my weight should be.
PETRUCHIO: Should be! should – buzz!
KATHARINA: Well ta'en, and like a **buzzard**.
PETRUCHIO: O slow-wing'd turtle! shall a **buzzard** take thee?
KATHARINA: Ay, for a turtle, as he takes a **buzzard**.

The other mention comes from Hastings, just released from imprisonment in the Tower of London, to Gloster (*King Richard III*, I, i, 132):

More pity that the eagle should be mew'd,
While kites and **buzzards** prey at liberty.

[30]

Whereupon Gloster abruptly changes the awkward subject with the little question, 'What news abroad?'

CACODEMON

Again it is in *King Richard III* that old Queen Margaret, that past-mistress in the art of vituperation, comes away with this balefully splendid word for Gloster, when she rounds upon the bloody rogue who had killed her husband and not a few of her other close relatives (I, iii, 143):

> Hie thee to hell for shame, and leave this world,
> Thou **cacodemon**! there thy kingdom is.

Gloster himself had just come away with a line of his own which touches just about the high-water mark of his gloating hypocrisy and smiling villainy, 'I am too childish-foolish for this world.'

The word Cacodemon is Greek for an evil spirit; and it sounds like one.

CALIBAN

There are two remarkable facts about Caliban, the monster in *The Tempest*, which are never sufficiently dwelt upon. One is that it is an exceedingly small part – barely 180 lines in all – to have made so tremendous an impact. The other is that he is a character who speaks nothing but blank verse, even in his several scenes with two clowns, a jester and a butler, who speak nothing but prose. This second fact we owe to the observation of Schlegel, the German critic, who made the first German translation of Shakespeare's plays.

Another extraordinary circumstance about this character is that we get only the vaguest inklings about what happens to him when the play is ended. We suppose – but are given no good reasons for supposing – that he is left on the island, which anyhow he regards as his own property. Prospero's last word to him is little more than a command to go home and tidy up (v, i, 291):

> Go, sirrah, to my cell;
> Take with you your companions; as you look
> To have my pardon, trim it handsomely.

And Caliban's last word before he goes is hardly conclusive, though it suggests that he is transferring his loyalty from Trinculo and Stephano back to Prospero (v, i, 294):

> Ay, that I will; and I'll be wise hereafter,
> And seek for grace. What a thrice-double ass
> Was I, to take this drunkard for a god,
> And worship this dull fool!

But we are never to know whether he found his grace, his conscience, or his soul.

Prospero and Ariel between them have already given us Caliban's pedigree. His father was a half-god and half-devil called Setebos, whom Patagonian Indians are said to have worshipped. His mother was 'the foul witch Sycorax', whom Prospero describes as a 'blue-eyed hag', though one is inclined to prefer the emendation of the adjective to 'blear-eyed'. It is Prospero too who describes him as he was in the beginning (I, ii, 283):

> A freckled whelp hag-born – not honour'd with
> A human shape.

See also MONSTERS IN GENERAL.

CAMELS

In the great soliloquy that turns into his swan song, Richard II curiously misquotes Holy Scripture (*King Richard II*, v, v, 15):

> As thus, 'Come, little ones;' and then again,
> 'It is as hard to come as for a **camel**
> To thread the postern of a needle's eye.'

This is very odd, and no scholar has any comment. Nothing whatever about the rich man's difficulty in getting into Heaven!

Elsewhere the camel is just the symbol of a beast of burden, as when Pandarus (*Troilus and Cressida*, I, ii, 251) says, 'Achilles! a drayman, a porter, a very **camel**.' To which Cressida comments, 'Well, well.'

There is also that cloud said to be shaped like a camel in *Hamlet* where Polonius is humouring the mad Prince, saying, 'By th' mass, and 'tis like a **camel**, indeed' (III, ii, 395).

CATERPILLARS

> Where is the Earl of Wiltshire? where is Bagot?
> What is become of Bushy? where is Green?

asks King Richard II about his favourites when he is nearing his own piteous end (*King Richard II*, III, ii, 122).

Not long before this we have heard these same favourites scornfully described by Bolingbroke (II, iii, 166) as:

> The **caterpillars** of the commonwealth,
> Which I have sworn to weed and pluck away.

And not long after, a politically-minded gardener's boy tells his master (III, iv, 44) that the whole land

Is full of weeds; her fairest flowers choked up,
Her fruit-trees all unpruned, her hedges ruin'd,
Her knots disorder'd, and her wholesome herbs
Swarming with **caterpillars**.

Whereon his even more politically-minded boss points the parallel (III, iv, 47):

Hold thy peace:
He that hath suffer'd this disorder'd spring
Hath now himself met with the fall of leaf:
The weeds that his broad-spreading leaves did shelter,
That seem'd in eating him to hold him up,
A **re** pluckt up root and all by Bolingbroke;
Imean the Earl of Wiltshire, Bushy, Green.

The same figure of speech is used twice in *King Henry VI, Part Two*. First, where the Duke of York has an aside on hearing of territories lost in France (III, i, 89):

Thus are my blossoms blasted in the bud,
And **caterpillars** eat my leaves away:
But I will remedy this gear ere long,
Or sell my title for a glorious grave.

And again, when a Messenger tells the King himself of the approach of Jack Cade and his rebel army in Southwark (IV, iv, 32):

His army is a ragged multitude
Of hinds and peasants, rude and merciless: ...
All scholars, lawyers, courtiers, gentlemen,
They call false **caterpillars**, and intend their death.

CATS AND POLECATS

Cats provide their own concert. Let us be content, for the nonce, with three fantastic quartets and some very out-of-the-way solos.

First the solos. 'The **cat,** with eyne of burning coal, Now couches fore the mouse's hole,' are two lines in a nocturne by Gower the Chorus in *Pericles* (Act III, Prologue, line 5). In the poems Tarquin is said to play cat-and-mouse with Lucrece (lines 554–555):

> Yet, foul night-waking **cat,** he doth but dally,
> While in his hold-fast foot the weak mouse panteth.

And Launce in *The Two Gentlemen of Verona* tells Crab, his dog, what an upset there was when he left home to make his fortune (II, iii, 6):

> ... my mother weeping, my father wailing, my sister crying, our maid howling, our **cat** wringing her hands, and all our house in a great perplexity, ...

Second, the quartets. Mercutio in *Romeo and Juliet* (III, i, 100) calls Tybalt, who has just given him his death-wound, four animals in a row – 'A plague o' both your houses! Zounds, a dog, a rat, a mouse, a **cat,** to scratch a man to death!'

And among the 'deal of skimble-skamble stuff' with which Owen Glendower has been boring Hotspur are, as the latter tells us in *King Henry IV, Part One,* III, i, 150, 'a clip-wing'd griffin and a moulten raven, a couching lion and a ramping **cat**'.

Polecats? Mistress Quickly hears from Master William Page what she takes to be a mention of polecats in *The Merry Wives of Windsor* (IV, i, 29) and says, '**Polecats!** there are fairer things than **polecats**, sure.' Whereupon the intensely Welsh Sir Hugh Evans rebukes her, 'You are a very simplicity 'oman: I pray you, peace.'

CENTAURS

Centaurs, according to the English and the mythological dictionaries, as well as the Elgin Marbles, were men down to the waist and horses below the waist. King Lear in his madness envisaged their top halves as feminine (*King Lear*, IV, vi, 124):

> Down from the waist they are **centaurs**,
> Though women all above,
> But to the girdle do the gods inherit,
> Beneath is all the fiends';

Grimmer still is the second-last scene of *Titus Andronicus*, where Titus, with his one remaining hand, slits the throats of the two sons of Tamora, who had ravished and mutilated Lavinia. He proposes to bake their heads and serve them up to Tamora as a banquet, and he spares us no detail of the recipe (V, ii, 197):

> . . . Lavinia, come,
> Receive the blood: and when that they are dead,
> Let me go grind their bones to powder small,
> And with this hateful liquor temper it;
> And in that paste let their vile heads be baked.
> Come, come, be every one officious
> To make this banquet; which I wish may prove
> More stern and bloody than the **Centaurs'** feast.

It is a pleasure to turn away from this bloody kitchen scene and point out that The Centaur was the name of the inn at Ephesus where much of the action of *The Comedy of Errors* takes place. Also that 'The Battle of the Centaurs' was one

of the *divertissements* offered to Theseus and Hippolyta for
their wedding feast at the end of *A Midsummer Night's
Dream* (v, i, 44). Theseus declined it, even though it was
'to be sung by an Athenian eunuch to the harp'.

CERBERUS

There are several allusions to Cerberus, the three-headed dog
which guarded the gate of Hell in Greek mythology. It pre-
vented the living from entering the infernal regions, and also
the dead from escaping their confinement.

In *Love's Labour's Lost* the little page, Moth, is cast for
Hercules in the elaborate masque within the play (v, ii, 581)
and is so announced by the pedant, Holofernes:

> Great Hercules is presented by this imp,
> Whose club kill'd **Cerberus**, that three-headed canis; . . .

In *Troilus and Cressida* the snarling Thersites rebukes Ajax
(II, i, 31):

> Thou grumblest and railest every hour on Achilles;
> and thou art as full of envy at his greatness as
> **Cerberus** is at Proserpina's beauty, ay, that thou
> bark'st at him.

In *Titus Andronicus* the mutilated Lavinia is met in the forest
by her uncle, Marcus Andronicus, who says of the unknown
despoiler (II, iv, 48):

> . . . had he heard the heavenly harmony
> Which that sweet tongue of thine hath often made,
> He would have dropt his knife, and fell asleep
> As **Cerberus** at the Thracian poet's feet.

But which of the Greek poets came from Thrace, which is
approximately the modern Roumania?

CHAMELEON

Not much less horrible is the *Oxford English Dictionary*'s definition of the Chameleon: 'a saurian reptile, of the genus *Chamaeleo*, distinguished by a prehensile tail, long tongue, eyes moving independently, but especially by their power of changing the colour of the skin, varying through different shades of yellow, red, gray, brown, and dull inky blue'.

King Claudius, at the beginning of the Play Scene, says, 'How fares our cousin Hamlet?' to get the mad answer:

> Excellent, i' faith, of the **chameleon's** dish: I eat
> the air, promise-cramm'd: you cannot feed capons so.

The King replies, 'I have nothing with this answer, Hamlet' (*Hamlet*, III, ii, 94). But the King may be supposed, perhaps, to be unaware of the old legend that the chameleon lived on air.

Similarly in *The Two Gentlemen of Verona* the clownish servant, Speed, hints to his master, Valentine, that he wants his dinner (II, i, 165), 'Though the **chameleon** Love can feed on the air, I am one that am nourish'd by my victuals, and would fain have meat.' There is a reference to another of the creature's *outré* habits in a later scene in the same play (II, iv, 23):

SILVIA: What, angry, Sir Thurio? do you change colour?
VALENTINE: Give him leave, madam; he is a kind of **chameleon**.

And there is a final reference to the creature's changeability of colour in Gloster's long solo in *King Henry VI, Part Three* (III, ii, 191). It is that same speech which Olivier interpolated, in his film version of *King Richard III*, into the opening soliloquy. Copying it out, one can hear again the great actor's precise enunciation of every vowel and consonant, and reflect between the lines, that the performance as a whole recalls the Dictionary's definition of the chameleon itself:

> I can add colours to the **chameleon**;
> Change shapes with Proteus for advantages;
> And set the murderous Machiavel to school.
> Can I do this, and cannot get a crown?
> Tut, were it further off, I'll pluck it down.

The single word 'pluck' was like a sudden stab of steel.

COCK AND COCKEREL

For the most part the word 'cock' in Shakespeare simply means the male of the common domestic fowl, *Gallus domesticus*. This is the Cock that crows at break of day. In *King Henry V* it crows before the Battle of Agincourt: Chorus's Prologue to Act IV:

> The country **cocks** do crow, the clocks do toll,
> And the third hour of drowsy morning name.

In *King Richard III* it crows before the Battle of Bosworth Field when Ratcliff tells the ill-rested King (v, iii, 209):

> The early **village-cock**
> Hath twice done salutation to the morn;
> Your friends are up, and buckle on their armour.

In *King Lear* the fugitive Edgar hails his familiar, 'This is the foul fiend Flibbertigibbet; he begins at curfew, and walks till the first **cock**' (III, iv, 114).

In this same sense of the word, Horatio and the officers of the watch in the first act of *Hamlet* may be described as 'cock-ridden'. Within a dozen lines (I, i, 147) Bernardo says of the Ghost, 'It was about to speak when the **cock** crew.' Horatio tells us:

> I have heard,
> The **cock**, that is the trumpet to the morn,
> Doth with his lofty and shrill-sounding throat
> Awake the god of day; and at his warning . . .
> Th' extravagant and erring spirit hies
> To his confine: . . .

And Marcellus says:

> It faded on the crowing of the **cock**.
> Some say, that ever 'gainst that season comes
> Wherein our Saviour's birth is celebrated,
> The bird of dawning singeth all night long: . . .

And it is presumably from the private parts of the same fowl's lusty offspring that Juliet's Nurse draws her simile when describing how once upon a time the baby fell on her face, as a result of which (*Romeo and Juliet*, I, iii, 53)

> . . . I warrant, it had upon its brow
> A bump as big as a young **cockerel's** stone.

Jaques in *As You Like It* (II, vii, 30) tells of an occasion when Touchstone amused him greatly, so that 'my lungs began to crow like **chanticleer**'. And Ariel concludes the song, 'Come unto these yellow sands' in *The Tempest* (I, ii, 384) with the lines:

> Hark, hark! I hear
> The strain of strutting **chanticleer**
> Cry, Cock-a-diddle dow.

All these – and some others could be given – are so many references to *Gallus domesticus*, the male of the common domestic fowl.

But it is no such thing as the male fowl which bobs up in one of poor Ophelia's mad ditties. It is, rather, the male *member*, and one had better say so in this permissive day and age when frankness is so much the fashion (*Hamlet*, IV, v, 57):

> By Gis and by Saint Charity,
>   Alack, and fie for shame!
> Young men will do't, if they come to't;
>   By **cock**, they are to blame.
> Quoth she, before you tumbled me,
>   You promised me to wed.
> So would I ha' done, by yonder sun,
>   An thou hadst not come to my bed.

CORMORANT

Once upon a time one joined an amused crowd of Dubliners on a bridge over the River Liffey. They were watching a cormorant on the surface of the water. It was 'afther swallowin' an eel' at one gulp, and could not get it down for quite a time.

The Cormorant (*Phalacrocorax carbo*) is a huge sea-bird which was probably never seen by Shakespeare, though its reputation for voracity and greed certainly reached him. He uses the word only figuratively, sometimes as a noun and sometimes as an adjective.

Thus the King of Navarre in his opening speech in *Love's Labour's Lost* (I, i, 4) talks of '**cormorant** devouring Time'. And Nestor in a letter to Priam in *Troilus and Cressida* (II, ii, 6) has a reference to 'this **cormorant** war'. Vanity is called an 'insatiate **cormorant**' by John of Gaunt in *King Richard II* (II, i, 38). And in *Coriolanus* (I, i, 118) the First Citizen, in his curious colloquy with Menenius about the Human Belly and its strength and its weaknesses, describes that organ as 'the **cormorant** belly', and describes it furthermore as 'the sink o' the body'.

[41]

COW AND CALF

The Cow is the female of any bovine animal. It has never been satisfactorily explained why any woman must resent being called a cow, a bitch, a she-cat, a mare, a vixen, etc., whereas hardly any man would find it either abusive or offensive to be called a bull, a dog, a tom-cat, or a stallion. But this is by the way.

In *Antony and Cleopatra* it is Enobarbus' friend, Scarus, who dares to call Cleopatra a cow, but only behind her back and as a figure of speech. He is raging with anger at the flight of Cleopatra and Antony from the sea-fight at Actium when he uses the phrase (III, x, 14):

> Yon ribaudred nag of Egypt . . .
> The breese [gad-fly] upon her, like a **cow** in June,
> Hoists sails and flies.

Most other references in the plays are purely to the animal, as when Touchstone in *As You Like It* reminisces about one Jane Smile, presumably a former Audrey, and 'the **cow's** dugs that her pretty chopt hands had milkt' (II, iv, 46). And a very minor character called Second Goth in *Titus Andronicus* has an odd observation that is positively Mendelian concerning the blackness of the baby that the white Tamora, Queen of the Goths, bore to the blackamoor Aaron (v, i, 31):

> . . . where the bull and **cow** are both milk-white,
> They never do beget a coal-black calf.

As for the Calf so begotten, and of whatsoever colour, let us record only one of several mentions. This is the one in *Love's Labour's Lost* in a scene between Longaville and Katherine during the masquerade (v, ii, 247) – one of those interchanges which one would sooner transcribe than try to explain:

KATHERINE: Veal, quoth the Dutchman. Is not 'veal' a **calf**?
LONGAVILLE: A **calf**, fair lady?
KATHERINE: No, a fair lord **calf**.
LONGAVILLE: Let's part the word.
KATHERINE: No, I'll not be your half:
  Take all, and wean it, it may prove an ox.
LONGAVILLE: Look, how you butt yourself in these sharp mocks!
  Will you give horns, chaste lady? do not so.
KATHERINE: Then die a **calf**, before your horns do grow.
LONGAVILLE: One word in private with you, ere I die.
KATHERINE: Bleat softly then; the butcher hears you cry.

Fooling at its heaviest!

CRABS AND PRAWNS

By 'crab' Shakespeare almost always means not the crustacean crab but rather the 'crab apple'. Foolishly, being rather an anti-scholar than a scholar worthy of the name, one had hitherto imagined that the Winter Song at the end of *Love's Labour's Lost* had a cheerful reference to boiled crab as a supper dish (v, ii, 912):

> When roasted **crabs** hiss in the bowl,
> Then nightly sings the staring owl,
>   Tu-who, tu-whit, tu-who.

But one now finds that Editor Hudson set us right about this as long ago as Edwardian times, when he provided the following delightful note, which really ought to have been quoted in the first volume of this series under APPLE:

This is the **crab apple**, which used to be roasted, and put hissing-hot

[43]

into a bowl of ale, previously enriched with toast and spice and sugar. How much this was relished in old times may be guessed by those who appreciate the virtues of apple-toddy.

But at least Hamlet must have meant the crustacean (*Cancer pagurus*) and not the wild apple when he remarked to Polonius (*Hamlet*, ii, ii, 200), 'For yourself, sir, shall grow old as I am, if, like a **crab,** you could go backward.' It is not really an intelligible remark: for Hamlet is here being mad rather than intelligible. But it is a fact that the crustacean in question can move in any direction – forwards, backwards, and (especially) sideways.

Prawns are much less equivocal and more straightforward. But here there is only a single reference to be discovered. It is buried in an immense prose-speech to Falstaff of Mistress Quickly – garrulous and breathless as Mrs Nickleby in Dickens – in *King Henry IV, Part Two* (ii, i, 80):

Thou didst swear to me upon a parcel-gilt goblet, sitting in my Dolphin-chamber, at the round table, by a sea-coal fire, upon Wednesday in Wheeson-week, when the prince broke thy head for liking his father to a singing-man of Windsor, – thou didst swear to me then, as I was washing thy wound, to marry me, and make me my lady thy wife. Canst thou deny it? Did not goodwife Keech, the butcher's wife, come in then, and call me gossip Quickly? coming in to borrow a mess of vinegar; telling us she had a good dish of **prawns**; whereby thou didst desire to eat some; whereby I told thee they were ill for a green wound? And didst thou not, when she was gone down stairs, desire me to be no more so familiarity with such poor people; saying that ere long they should call me madam? And didst thou not kiss me, and bid me fetch thee thirty shillings? I put thee now to thy book-oath: deny it, if thou canst.

That these were prawns (*Palaemon senatus*) is as undeniable as Falstaff found Mistress Quickly's evidence.

CUCKOOS

The Cuckoo (*Cuculus manorus*) lays its eggs and has them hatched in the nests of other birds. For this reason – though it may not be a strictly logical reason – it is from the word 'cuckoo' that the once-common term 'cuckold' is directly derived. A cuckold, according to the *Oxford English Dictionary*, was – and is still – a husband whose wife is unfaithful to him with one or more other men. The word, it seems, applies only to the deceived husband, never to a deceived wife (surely quite as common a phenomenon?). The *O.E.D.* goes out of its way to add to its definition the comment, 'In English *cuckold* is not found applied to the adulterer.'

There seems much loose thinking and loose argument about this complicated etymology (though maybe there always is in sexual matters). One would only point out that the cuckoo bird – a hen, of course – is guilty not of infidelity but of sheer laziness when it lays its eggs in another bird's nest. The trouble is that we simply don't know enough about the domestic – or, rather, the non-domestic – life of a cuckoo couple. Are they more, or less, faithful than other bird couples? Is the cock cuckoo ever a cuckold?

Another oddity about the *O.E.D.*'s definition is that it declares the word to be 'derisory'. But is there anything less 'derisory' than Othello's use of the word about himself (*Othello*, IV, i, 198)? Othello is quite wrong about his cuckolding. But that is beside the point:

OTHELLO: I will chop her into messes! **cuckold** me!
IAGO: O, 'tis foul in her.
OTHELLO: With mine officer!
IAGO: That's fouler.
OTHELLO: Get me some poison, Iago; this night: – I'll not expostulate

with her, lest her body and beauty unprovide my mind again; –
this night, Iago.

IAGO: Do it not with poison, strangle her in her bed, even the bed
she hath contaminated.

There is no more terrifying, or less derisory, passage in the
whole tragedy.

References in Shakespeare to the Cuckoo, without these
adulterous overtones and double meanings, are few but all the
more welcome. Thus, Portia is recognized by Lorenzo in the
garden at Belmont by night (*The Merchant of Venice*, v, i, 110):

LORENZO:　　　　　　That is the voice,
　Or I am much deceived, of Portia.
PORTIA: He knows me, as the blind man knows the **cuckoo**,
　By the bad voice.

And the Fool's snatch of verse, amid the terrible scene
between King Lear and his daughter Goneril (*King Lear*, I, iv,
212), indicates that Shakespeare was well aware of the Cuckoo's life-history and habits:

> The hedge-sparrow fed the **cuckoo** so long,
> That it had it head bit off by **it young**.

CYCLOPS

Mythology tells us that the Cyclopes were one-eyed giant
blacksmiths who forged thunderbolts for the use of the gods.
They were said to have worked for Vulcan in the vicinity of
Mount Etna.

The First Player, giving Hamlet a taste of his quality in
tragedy, has a striking allusion to them (*Hamlet*, II, ii, 488):

> And never did the **Cyclops'** hammers fall
> On Mars's armour, forg'd for proof eterne,

> With less remorse than Pyrrhus' bleeding sword
> Now falls on Priam.

And Titus Andronicus says to his own brother (*Titus Andronicus*, IV, iii, 45):

> Marcus, we are but shrubs, no cedars we,
> No big-boned men framed of the **Cyclops'** size;
> But metal, Marcus, steel to the very back,
> Yet wrung with wrongs more than our backs can bear.

This present commentator did once set eyes – both eyes – on a real-life Cyclops. He was a beggar-man in Istanbul. He was of no great height. But he was apparently dumb, and he had a single, round, and rather red eye, set in the middle of his forehead, close to the top of his nose. He opened the door of my taxi and mutely held out his hand for a coin, which was very quickly forthcoming. The British Council representative by my side was no less shocked, scared, and speedily generous.

DEER

Deer abound – and here we must be particularly selective. The aim now should be, as seemeth to me, to give one relishable, and not too familiar, example of the various forms and styles of Deer (of the order *Cervidae*), and to conclude with one or two particular *bonnes bouches* from the same source.

There is John Talbot, Earl of Shrewsbury, in *King Henry VI, Part One* (IV, ii, 45), though the allusion is only to his own troops:

> How are we parkt and bounded in a pale,
> A little herd of England's timorous **deer**.

There is Mrs Ford at the end of *The Merry Wives of Windsor* and in Windsor Park telling Falstaff that all is over between them (v, v, 114), 'Sir John we have had ill luck; we could never meet. I will never take you for my love again; but I will always count you my **deer** [so spelt].'

There is the Exiled Duke in *As You Like It* commenting on the philosopher Jaques (II, i, 64):

DUKE: And did you leave him in this contemplation?
SECOND LORD: We did, my lord, weeping and commenting
   Upon the sobbing **deer**.
DUKE: Show me the place:
   I love to cope him in these sullen fits,
   For then he's full of matter.
FIRST LORD: I'll bring you to him straight.

There is Mark Antony over Caesar's corpse (*Julius Caesar*, III, i, 208):

      O world! thou wast the forest to this **hart**;
      And this, indeed, O world, the heart of thee.
      How like a **deer**, strucken by many princes,
      Dost thou here lie!

There is Hamlet in his frenzy of excitement at the end of the Play Scene (*Hamlet*, III, ii, 290):

      Why, let the stricken **deer** go weep,
         The **hart** ungalled play;
      For some must watch, while some must sleep:
         So runs the world away.

There is Orlando, demanding food with drawn sword, and saying he must first succour his old servant Adam (*As You Like It*, II, vii, 127):

      Then but forbear your food a little while,
      Whiles, like a **doe**, I go to find my **fawn**,
      And give it food.

There is Octavius on Antony's service-fare in *Antony and Cleopatra* (I, iv, 63):

> ... Thy palate then did deign
> The roughest berry in the rudest hedge;
> Yea, like the **stag**, when snow the pasture sheets,
> The barks of trees thou browsed'st; ...

There is Page to Mistress Page in *The Merry Wives of Windsor* (I, i, 177):

> Wife, bid these gentlemen welcome. Come, we have a hot **venison**-pasty to dinner; come, gentlemen, I hope we shall drink down all unkindness.

DEVILS

One may make a rising crescendo out of only ten of the innumerable references –

Armado in *Love's Labour's Lost* (I, ii, 165): 'Love is a familiar; Love is a **devil**: there is no evil angel but love.'

Hotspur to Lady Hotspur in *King Henry IV, Part One* (III, i, 228): 'Now I perceive the **devil** understands Welsh.'

Theseus on the madman in *A Midsummer Night's Dream* (V, i, 9): 'One sees more **devils** than vast hell can hold.'

Lady Anne to Gloster in *King Richard III* (I, ii, 50): 'Foul **devil**, for God's sake, hence, and trouble us not.'

Lucrece on Tarquin (line 1555): 'Such **devils** steal effects from lightless hell.'

Ferdinand, leaping ashore from the shipwreck in *The Tempest* (I, ii, 215): 'Hell is empty, And all the **devils** are here.'

Macbeth to his Lady asking if he is still a man (*Macbeth* III, iv, 59): 'Ay, and a bold one, that dare look on that Which might appal the **devil**.'

Prospero to Caliban in *The Tempest* (I, ii, 319): 'Thou poisonous slave, got by the **devil** himself, Upon thy wicked dam.'

Clown to Lafeu in *All's Well That Ends Well* (IV, v, 39): 'The black prince, sir; *alias*, the prince of darkness, *alias*, the **devil**.'

Lear fleeing from Goneril in *King Lear* (I, iv, 257): 'Darkness and **devils**!'

DOGS

One of the supreme things in Olivier's great Macbeth was the scene with the murderers he has hired to slay Banquo and Banquo's young son, Fleance. The First Murderer protests, 'We are men, my liege', and it is the cue for the tyrant's withering rejoinder which many a Macbeth in our time has thrown away. Not so Olivier, who loaded the lines with irony as well as scorn, his Macbeth being one who already felt his secret murders sticking on his hands (III, i, 91):

> Ay, in the catalogue ye go for men;
> As hounds, and greyhounds, mongrels, spaniels, curs,
> Shoughs, water-rugs, and demi-wolves, are clept
> All by the name of **dogs**: the valued file
> Distinguishes the swift, the slow, the subtle,
> The housekeeper, the hunter, every one
> According to the gift which bounteous nature
> Hath in him closed; whereby he does receive
> Particular addition, from the bill
> That writes them all alike: and so of men.
> Now, if ye have a station in the file,
> Not i' th' worst rank of manhood, say't;
> And I will put that business in your bosoms,
> Whose execution takes your enemy off,

Grapples you to the heart and love of us,
Who wear our health but sickly in his life,
Which in his death were perfect.

Edgar, the pretended madman in *King Lear* (III, vi, 63), has a less enthralling catalogue of dogs, but it is complementary to Macbeth's:

Avaunt, you **curs**!
Be thy mouth or black or white,
Tooth that poisons if it bite;
Mastiff, greyhound, mongrel grim,
Hound or spaniel, brach or lym,
Or bobtail tike or trundle-tail;
Tom will make them weep and wail:
For, with throwing thus my head,
Dogs leap the hatch, and all are fled.

Of actual dogs, appearing or mentioned in the plays, there is in *The Two Gentlemen of Verona* (II, iii, 5) 'the sourest-natured **dog** that lives' – Launce's dog, Crab. There are King Lear's little dogs, Tray, Blanch and Sweetheart, which bark at him; there is also in the same play the Fool's 'brach' or **scent-hound** called Lady, which does nothing but 'stand by the fire and stink' (I, iv, 115). Hotspur, in *King Henry IV, Part One*, has another **scent-hound** called Lady which he would like to hear 'howl in Irish'.

The Hunting Lord in the Induction to *The Taming of the Shrew* mentions some of his hounds by name – Merriman, Clowder, Silver, Belman and Echo. Of all these it is only Launce's dog, Crab, which actually appears – when it invariably runs away with the play, what there is of it.

DOLPHIN AND PORPOISE

Cleopatra does nobly by the Dolphin when she makes mention of it in connection with the dead Antony and his pleasures when alive (*Antony and Cleopatra*, v, ii, 86):

> ... For his bounty,
> There was no winter in't; an autumn 'twas
> That grew the more by reaping: his delights
> Were **dolphin**-like; they show'd his back above
> The element they lived in: ...

In its other two significant mentions the Dolphin is cavorting at sea with a passenger bestriding it. Thus Oberon in *A Midsummer Night's Dream* (ii, i, 149) tells his gentle Puck:

> ... once I sat upon a promontory,
> And heard a mermaid, on a **dolphin's** back,
> Uttering such dulcet and harmonious breath,
> That the rude sea grew civil at her song, ...

And then the Captain in *Twelfth Night* (i, ii, 14) tells Viola of her lost brother, Sebastian, that he was seen binding himself

> To a strong mast that lived upon the sea;
> Where, like Arion on the **dolphin's** back,
> I saw him hold acquaintance with the waves
> So long as I could see.

The Dolphin is described by biologists as a cetacean mammal. So, too, is the no less playful porpoise which appears with the old name of 'porpus' and has only a single mention. This is at the opening of the second act of *Pericles, Prince of Tyre*, when that wandering hero is thrown up by the sea on the shore at Pentapolis and found by three fishermen (ii, i, 20):

FIRST FISHERMAN: Alas, poor souls, it grieved my heart to hear what pitiful cries they made to us to help them, when, well-a-day, we could scarce help ourselves.

THIRD FISHERMAN: Nay, master, said not I as much when I saw the **porpus,** how he bounced and tumbled? they say they're half-fish, half-flesh: . . .

DOVES AND PIGEONS

Hermia in *A Midsummer Night's Dream* (I, i, 171) swears very prettily 'by the simplicity of Venus' **doves**'.

Juliet's Nurse in *Romeo and Juliet* (I, iii, 27) tells how she was once 'sitting in the sun under the **dove-house** wall'.

Perdita in *The Winter's Tale* (IV, iii, 367) is told that her hand is 'as soft as **dove's** down, and as white as it'.

Gertrude after Ophelia's funeral and at the end of Hamlet's rant by the grave (*Hamlet*, V, i, 278) has her strange and lovely speech:

> This is mere madness:
> And thus awhile the fit will work on him;
> Anon, as patient as the female **dove**
> When that her golden couplets are disclosed,
> His silence will sit drooping.

Paris in *Troilus and Cressida* (III, i, 122) exclaims to Helen (and sounds much more like Pandarus as he does so): 'He eats nothing but **doves**, love; and that breeds hot blood, and hot blood begets hot thoughts, and hot thoughts beget hot deeds, and hot deeds is love.'

These are but a few of the references to the Dove, incessant as his cooing. Two references to the Pigeon, as distinct from the Dove, are much less passionate and much more prosaic. They occur respectively in *Love's Labour's Lost* (V, ii, 315) and *King Henry IV, Part Two* (V, i, 23). They are Berowne's 'This fellow pecks up wit as **pigeons** pease,' and Justice Shallow's order to his servant while entertaining Falstaff in Gloucestershire, 'Some **pigeons**, Davy, a couple of short-legg'd hens, a joint of mutton, and any pretty little tiny kickshaws, tell William cook.'

DRAGONS

A Dragon contributes one of its scales to the Witches' Brew in *Macbeth* (IV, i, 22), and 'a **dragon** and a finless fish' are among the properties of Glendower which Hotspur finds so tedious in *King Henry IV, Part One* (III, i, 150).

But the most interesting usages of the word are less direct and more symbolic, and spring from what is apparently self-knowledge. 'Come not between the **dragon** and his wrath,' says King Lear to Kent, when the latter tries to interfere with the old man's unjust spurning of Cordelia (I, i, 122). But another character in the same play who has far more of genuine self-knowedge is Gloster's natural son, Edmund, who has no illusions whatever about heredity, and gives his conviction brilliant expression (*King Lear*, I, ii, 130) with a dragon dramatically participating:

An admirable evasion of whoremaster man, to lay his goatish disposition to the charge of a star! My father compounded with my mother under the **dragon's tail**; and my nativity was under *ursa major*; so that it follows, I am rough and lecherous. Fut, I should have been that I am, had the maidenliest star in the firmament twinkled on my bastardizing.

Coriolanus is twice likened to a dragon, once by himself, once by his friend Menenius. The great man addresses his friends and relatives in turn, concluding with Volumnia (*Coriolanus*, IV, i, 27):

My mother, you wot well
My hazards still have been your solace: and

> Believe't not lightly, though I go alone,
> Like to a lonely **dragon**, that his fen
> Makes fear'd and talkt of more than seen, . . .

Menenius in a later passage vividly describes Coriolanus near the end of the heyday of his pride (v, iv, 10):

MENENIUS: This Marcius is grown from man to **dragon**: he has wings; he's more than a creeping thing.

SICINIUS: He loved his mother dearly.

MENENIUS: But so did he me: and he no more remembers his mother now than an eight-year-old horse. The tartness of his face sours ripe grapes: when he walks, he moves like an engine, and the ground shrinks before his treading: . . . He sits in his state, as a thing made for Alexander. What he bids be done, is finisht with his bidding. He wants nothing of a god but eternity, and a heaven to throne in. . . . I paint him in the character. Mark what mercy his mother shall bring from him: there is no more mercy in him than there is milk in a male tiger.

DUCK AND MALLARD

Almost the only mention of the Duck (*Anas*), excepting in its secondary sense as a term of endearment, is in *The Tempest*. It is in a marvellously characterized little scene between Caliban and the butler Stephano and the jester Trinculo, the latter two having just been reunited after the shipwreck (II, ii, 112):

CALIBAN (*aside*): These be fine things, an if they be not sprites.
That's a brave god, and bears celestial liquor:
I will kneel to him.

STEPHANO: How didst thou 'scape? How camest thou hither? swear, by this bottle, how thou camest hither. I escaped upon a butt of sack, which the sailors heaved o'erboard, by this bottle! which I made of the bark of a tree with mine own hands, since I was cast ashore.

CALIBAN: I'll swear, upon that bottle, to be thy true subject, for the liquor is not earthly.

STEPHANO: Here; swear, then, how thou escapedst.

TRINCULO: Swam ashore, man, like a **duck**: I can swim like a **duck**, I'll be sworn.

STEPHANO: Here, kiss the book. Though thou canst swim like a **duck**, thou art made like a goose.

TRINCULO: O Stephano, hast any more of this?

STEPHANO: The whole butt, man: my cellar is in a rock by the sea-side, where my wine is hid. – How now, moon-calf! how does thine ague?

CALIBAN: Hast thou not dropt from heaven?

STEPHANO: Out o' the moon, I do assure thee: I was the man-i'-the-moon when time was.

CALIBAN: I've seen thee in her, and I do adore thee.

Such scenes ought to 'come off' in the theatre better than they usually do. They are simple in language (unlike similar scenes of fooling in, for example, *Twelfth Night* and *As You Like It*). They even have a positively 'pop' flavour with the foolishly repetitive 'man', but still they *read* much better than they usually *act*.

The Mallard or wild duck (*Anas boscas*) gets only a solitary quack, though it is in surely the greatest and largest of all the plays, *Antony and Cleopatra*. The queen is seized with panic and flies from the sea-fight at Actium, closely followed by Antony, to the disgust of Scarus (III, x, 20) who says that Antony has behaved 'like a doting **mallard**'.

EAGLE

The Eagle (*Aquila*), the royal bird, can easily provide us with a dozen lofty images. Some of the best are some of the least familiar. Thus Warwick, dying at the Battle of Barnet (*King Henry VI, Part Three*, v, ii, 11):

> Thus yields the cedar to the axe's edge,
> Whose arms gave shelter to the princely **eagle**, . . .
> Why, what is pomp, rule, reign, but earth and dust?
> And, live we how we can, yet die we must.

And thus Philip Falconbridge speaks to the French on behalf of the English king in *King John* (v, ii, 148):

> . . . Know the gallant monarch is in arms,
> And, like an **eagle** o'er his aery, towers,
> To souse annoyance that comes near his nest.

And thus the Earl of Westmoreland reminds his king how the Scots customarily behave when the English back is turned on them as they face France (*King Henry V*, 1, ii, 169):

> For once the **eagle** England being in prey,
> To her unguarded nest the weasel Scot
> Comes sneaking, and so sucks her princely eggs;
> Playing the mouse in absence of the cat,
> To spoil and havoc more than she can eat.

And Gloster, more familiarly but with irresistible *diablerie*, assumes a virtue when he has it not (*King Richard III*, 1, iii, 70):

> I cannot tell: the world is grown so bad,
> That wrens may prey where **eagles** dare not perch:
> Since every Jack became a gentleman,
> There's many a gentle person made a Jack.

The rest of the military parade are as nothing to Pandarus when Troilus has passed in the procession (*Troilus and Cressida*, 1, ii, 239) and his speech to Cressida, even with its repeated phrases, is intensely characteristic:

Asses, fools, dolts! chaff and bran, chaff and bran! porridge after meat! I could live and die i' th' eyes of Troilus. Ne'er look, ne'er look; the **eagles** are gone; crows and daws, crows and daws! I had rather be such a man as Troilus than Agamemnon and all Greece.

And near the end of *Cymbeline* (v, iv, 113) no less a god than Jupiter descends upon an eagle from Olympus, utters a fine oration in honour of Imogen, and ascends to Olympus again with the absolutely transcendent final line:

> Mount, **eagle**, to my palace crystalline.

EEL and CONGER

Marina, the daughter of Pericles, is a lost soul, but wanders unsullied and 'in strong proof of chastity well armed' (like Romeo's Rosaline). It is admittedly – as the workaday world would say – a very near thing when she finds herself in captivity in a brothel, and when she has to take part in this snatch of conversation with a Bawd (unnamed) and one Boult (who is a Pander's servant – as low a calling as one could come by). The play is *Pericles, Prince of Tyre* (IV, ii, 133):

BAWD: Come, young one, I like the manner of your garments well.
BOULT: Ay, by my faith, they shall not be changed yet.
BAWD: Boult, spend thou that in the town: report what a sojourner we have; you'll lose nothing by custom. When nature framed this piece, she meant thee a good turn; therefore say what a paragon she is, and thou hast the harvest out of thine own report.
BOULT: I warrant you, mistress, thunder shall not so awake the beds of **eels** as my giving out her beauty stir up the lewdly-inclined. I'll bring home some to-night.
BAWD: Come your ways, follow me.
MARINA: If fires be hot, knives sharp, or waters deep,
Untied I still my virgin knot will keep.
Diana, aid my purpose!
BAWD: What have we to do with Diana? Pray you, will you go with us?   [*Exeunt*

But the goddess – and Marina – had the last word all the same.
  Conger, the outsize in eels or sea-eels, has two mentions,

both in *King Henry IV, Part Two*. Doll Tearsheet calls Falstaff 'a muddy **conger**', while telling him to go and hang himself (II, iv, 54); and Falstaff tells Doll Tearsheet that the somewhat nondescript character called Pointz (II, iv, 243) plays quoits well and 'eats **conger** and fennel,' which is said to have been a high old mixture. Conger, incidentally, is a high old dish.

ELEPHANT

One of the conspirators against Caesar, Decius Brutus, has a remark to Cassius which indicates some grounding in elementary psychology (*Julius Caesar*, II, i, 202). Cassius has just been opining that several bad omens may prevent Caesar going to the Capitol on that fatal day. But Decius Brutus is firmly and shrewdly of the opposite opinion:

> Never fear that: if he be so resolved,
> I can o'ersway him; for he loves to hear
> That unicorns may be betray'd with trees,
> And bears with glasses, **elephants** with holes,
> Lions with toils, and men with flatterers:
> But when I tell him he hates flatterers,
> He says he does, being then most flattered.
> Let me work;
> And I will bring him to the Capitol.

The Elephant is the often-mentioned name of the inn 'in the south suburbs' in Illyria (*Twelfth Night*, III, iii, 39). But the animal itself is only referred to, figuratively, in one other play, *Troilus and Cressida*. Cressida hears Ajax described by her eloquent servant, Alexander, as being 'valiant as the lion, churlish as the bear, slow as the **elephant**' (I, ii, 20). The blunt-tongued Thersites bluntly calls the same character 'the **elephant** Ajax,' though behind his back (II, iii, 2). And later, within the same scene, Ulysses comes away – for no reason at all – with his own expression of the old legend that elephants never kneel or lie down: 'The **elephant** hath joints, but none for courtesy: his legs are legs for necessity, not for flexure' (II, iii, 99).

It is one's own observation that that much more familiar animal, the horse (which see), seldom lies down when well, and usually sleeps standing. Moreover, when a horse falls down by accident it cannot wait to get on all fours again, unless it be grievously hurt.

FALCON AND KITE

Both are of the falcon family (*Falconidae*). The Falcon, more fully the peregrine falcon, plays its part in the unnatural happenings in nature on the night of King Duncan's murder. An unnamed Old Man tells Ross (*Macbeth* II, iv, 12) how on the previous Tuesday –

> A **falcon**, towering in her pride of place,
> Was by a mousing owl hawk'd at and kill'd.

The same bird's assurance is cited by Bolingbroke in *King Richard II* (I, iii, 59):

> O, let no noble eye profane a tear
> For me, if I be gored with Mowbray's spear:
> As confident as is the **falcon's** flight
> Against a bird, do I with Mowbray fight.

Lord Clifford in *King Henry VI, Part Three* has an observation to the effect that even the most overpowered creature may still have a little game struggle left in it (I, iv, 40):

> So cowards fight when they can fly no further;
> So doves do peck the **falcon's** piercing talons;
> So desperate thieves, all hopeless of their lives,
> Breathe out invectives 'gainst the officers.

And Touchstone, in one of his too few colloquies with the philosopher Jaques, tells us how he is threatened with wedlock, and in passing mentions that falcons were supplied with bells, as they still are when one sees any (*As You Like It*, III, iii, 73):

JAQUES: Will you be married, motley?
TOUCHSTONE: As the ox hath his bow, sir, the horse his curb, and the **falcon** her bells, so man hath his desires; and as pigeons bill, so wedlock would be nibbling.

All the references to the Kite are much unpleasanter. Antony is clearly in a dangerous rage when he discovers Caesar's messenger bending over Cleopatra's hand (III, xiii, 89):

Approach, there! – Ah, you **kite**! – Now, gods and devils!
Authority melts from me: . . .

And Macbeth, facing the stare of the blood-boltered Banquo's ghost, is almost incoherent with terror (*Macbeth*, III, iv, 69):

Prithee, see there! behold! look! lo! how say you?
Why, what care I? If thou canst nod, speak too.
If charnel-houses and our graves must send
Those that we bury back, our monuments
Shall be the maws of **kites.**

A far from ideal Macbeth, Charles Laughton was unforgettable in this scene, and in this particular speech.

FIEND AND FLIBBERTIGIBBET

Gloster's son, Edgar, in his naked guise as Poor Tom (*King Lear*), more than once conjures up various fiends and familiars, the friendliest of which he calls Flibbertigibbet (III, iv, 118):

This is the foul **fiend Flibbertigibbet:** he begins at curfew, and walks till the first cock; he gives the web and the pin [= eye distempers], squints the eye, and makes the hare-lip; mildews the white wheat, and hurts the poor creature of earth.

Edgar has still worse company (III, iv, 145):

Beware my follower. Peace, Smulkin; peace, thou **fiend**! ... The prince of darkness is a gentleman: Modo he's called, and Mahu.

And, later, Edgar raves on and on to his father, who has been cruelly blinded and does not recognize him (IV, i, 59):

Poor Tom hath been scared out of his good wits: bless thee, good man's son, from the foul **fiend**! five **fiends** have been in poor Tom at once: of lust, as Obidicut; Hobbididence, prince of dumbness; Mahu, of stealing; Modo, of murder; and **Flibbertigibbet**, of mopping and mowing, who since possesses chambermaids and waiting-women. So, bless thee, master!

Fiends, more or less foul, swarm in Shakespeare, as in one of those proverb-canvases of Bosch or the elder Bruegel or Breugel (he spells it both ways). 'They are devils' additions, the names of **fiends**,' says Ford in *The Merry Wives of Windsor* (II, ii, 298). 'The **fiend** is at mine elbow, and tempts me,' says Launcelot Gobbo in *The Merchant of Venice* (II, ii, 2). 'Out, hyperbolical **fiend**! how vexest thou this man!' says Feste, when confronted with Malvolio, who is said to be mad and therefore possessed by a fiend (*Twelfth Night*, IV, ii, 27). '**Fiend**, thou torment'st me ere I come to hell!' says Richard II to Bolingbroke (*King Richard II*, IV, i, 270).

And so on, by the score. The marvel is that the most evil and pernicious character in all the plays, Iago, is nowhere called a fiend, either to his face or behind his back. Till the end he conceals his innate fiendishness only too well, not only from his master and mistress, but even from his wife Emilia; and it is perhaps Shakespeare's fault that he has made Emilia too shrewd a woman to have been deceived by that specious fiend for quite so long.

FISHES in GENERAL

Respecting fish, there is no lovelier image in all the plays than the one in the long poem *Venus and Adonis* (line 1099) where Venus envisages her shepherd bathing:

> When he beheld his shadow in the brook,
> The **fishes** spread on it their golden gills; . . .

But there are marvellous other effects in the plays. The effect sinister, as in Clarence's account of his under-water dream in *King Richard III* (I, iv, 24):

> Methought I saw a thousand fearful wrecks;
> Ten thousand men that **fishes** gnaw'd upon;
> Wedges of gold, great anchors, heaps of pearl,
> Inestimable stones, unvalued jewels,
> All scatt'red in the bottom of the sea: . . .

The effect philosophic, as in *Hamlet* in the Prince's rapid interchange with Claudius (IV, iii, 28):

HAMLET: A man may **fish** with the worm that hath eat of a king, and eat of the **fish** that hath fed of that worm.
KING: What dost thou mean by this?
HAMLET: Nothing but to show you how a king may go a progress through the guts of a beggar.

And the effect plainly comical, as when Trinculo comes upon the sleeping Caliban in *The Tempest* when another tempest seems imminent (II, ii, 20):

Yond same black cloud, yond huge one, looks like a foul bombard that would shed his liquor. If it should thunder as it did before, I know not where to hide my head: yond same cloud cannot choose but fall by pailfuls. What have we here? a man or a **fish**? dead or alive? A **fish**: he smells like a **fish**; a very ancient and **fish-like** smell; ...

And so Trinculo goes on and on till he arrives at a sentence which compensates us richly for his verbosity: 'Misery acquaints a man with strange bedfellows.'

FLEAS, FLIES AND GNATS

These again abound, and again one has to pick and choose – and scratch.

Petruchio with his wife's Tailor lets out a nice stream of dog's abuse in *The Taming of the Shrew* (IV, iii, 109): 'Thou **flea**, thou nit, thou winter-cricket thou!' Sir Toby tells Fabian what he thinks of Sir Andrew's valour, or lack of it, in *Twelfth Night* (III, ii, 50): 'For Andrew, if he were open'd, and you find so much blood in his liver as will clog the foot of a **flea**, I'll eat the rest of th' anatomy.' And in *King Henry V* the followers of Falstaff, after his death, indulge in affectionate reminiscence (II, iii, 42). The Boy says: 'Do you not remember, a' saw a **flea** stand upon Bardolph's nose, and a' said it was a black soul burning in hell-fire?' This usually wins a laugh in the theatre which drowns Bardolph's very characteristic answer: 'Well, the fuel is gone that maintain'd that fire: that's all the riches I got in his service.'

Around the subject of Flies, Lear's Gloster is absolute, Othello terrifying, and Cleopatra tremendous. Gloster (*King Lear*, IV, i, 37) declares:

> As **flies** to wanton boys, are we to the gods,
> They kill us for their sport.

Othello answers the doomed Desdemona's utterance, 'I hope

my noble lord esteems me honest,' in this sort (*Othello*, IV, ii, 66):

> O, ay; as summer **flies** are in the shambles,
> That quicken even with blowing.

And Cleopatra to Antony, just before they choose to have 'one other gaudy night', very nearly transcends language in the lines (*Antony and Cleopatra*, III, xiii, 161):

> . . . as it determines, so
> Dissolve my life! The next Caesarion smite!
> Till, by degrees, the memory of my womb,
> Together with my brave Egyptians all,
> By the discandying of this pelleted storm,
> Lie graveless, till the **flies** and **gnats** of Nile
> Have buried them for prey!

After this any Gnats of any sort must flutter in anti-climax – for example, those in *The Comedy of Errors*. In this observation of Antipholus of Syracuse (II, ii, 30) their behaviour is seen to be not very different from that of humankind:

> When the sun shines let foolish **gnats** make sport,
> But creep in crannies when he hides his beams.

FOWL AND WILDFOWL

In his superb answer to the psycho-analyst Feste, the locked-up Malvolio proves himself as right-minded as anybody else in *Twelfth Night* (IV, ii, 47):

MALVOLIO: I say, this house is as dark as ignorance, though ignorance were as dark as hell; and I say, there was never man thus abused. I am no more mad than you are: make the trial of it in any constant question.

FESTE: What is the opinion of Pythagoras concerning **wildfowl**?
MALVOLIO: That the soul of our grandam might haply inhabit a bird.
FESTE: What think'st thou of his opinion?
MALVOLIO: I think nobly of the soul, and no way approve his opinion.

In out-of-the-way places two haunting phrases about fowl should here be noted. The one is in the last scene of *Titus Andronicus* (v, iii, 67) where, with the stage strewn with bleeding corpses, Lucius Andronicus addresses the Romans:

> You sad-faced men, people and sons of Rome,
> By uproar sever'd, like a flight of **fowl**
> Scatter'd by winds and high tempestuous gusts,
> O, let me teach you . . .

The other is early on in the action of *Cymbeline*, when Iachimo is telling Posthumus that he need not be too complacent or cocksure about his wife Imogen's integrity and fidelity (I, iv, 87): 'You know, strange **fowl** light upon neighbouring ponds.' Here Shakespeare is being positively Strindbergian.

But these are unfamiliar things. Among the familiar ones, we simply cannot ignore that sublimely stupid leading man, Bottom, and his sensibility about scaring his audience with the sight and sound of a real lion (*A Midsummer Night's Dream*, III, i, 29): 'Masters, you ought to consider with yourselves: to bring in, – God shield us! – a lion among ladies is a most dreadful thing; for there is not a more fearful **wild-fowl** than your lion living; and we ought to look to't.'

FOX AND VIXEN

The Fox is famed for its craftiness and cunning, the Vixen solely for its short temper. The vixen is mentioned only in *A Midsummer Night's Dream* (III, ii, 323) where Helena com-

ments on Hermia who is sharper as well as shorter than herself:

> O, when she's angry, she is keen and shrewd!
> She was a **vixen** when she went to school;
> And though she be but little, she is fierce.

When Hermia protests warmly at this, Lysander adds insult
to the injury: 'Get you gone, you dwarf; You minimus, of
hind'ring knot-grass made; You bead, you acorn.'

But Shakespeare, oddly enough, has no mention of craft or
cunning in his many mentions of the fox. 'Subtle', in the old
sense of the word, is the nearest he comes to the traditional
attribute, and this is best instanced not in any of the plays but
in that lovely long poem, *Venus and Adonis*, which will never
belong to the popular taste because it is about frustration, not
gratification.

In an uninterrupted speech of more than a hundred lines
Venus has a flying reference to 'the **fox** which lives by
subtlety' (line 675). But Adonis, who would infinitely rather
hunt the boar than be bored by Venus, practically tells her so
to her importunate face (lines 773–774):

> For, by this black-faced night, desire's foul nurse,
> Your treatise makes me like you worse and worse.

FROGS AND TOADS

We are again in the world of reptilian familiars. They have
their liveliest orgy, both the living and the dead familiars, in
the opening scene of the fourth act of *Macbeth*. Some relegate
this scene to the cruder pen of Thomas Middleton. But those
who do so unthinkingly might like to reassess Middleton. He
may have been a much inferior playwright. He was. But he

was a far better dog at a title. Only an insane bias in favour of Shakespeare over all other Elizabethans and Jacobeans put together could make out that *Twelfth Night*, *As You Like It*, and *Much Ado About Nothing* are anything like such promising play-titles as *The Roaring Girl*, *A Chaste Maid in Cheapside*, and *A Mad World*, *My Masters*, which are plays by Middleton. (Pursuing this matter a step further, we may opine that *The Tempest* is a poor reach-me-down sort of title for what is perhaps the most magical and metaphysical fantasy ever written to be acted or merely read.)

The Frog (*Rana*) has an edible species, and the Toad (*Bufo*) has none such. But both come into the regular menu, with some other non-delicacies, of Edgar masquerading as Poor Tom in *King Lear* (III, iv, 132):

Poor Tom; that eats the swimming **frog**, the **toad**, the tadpole, the wall-newt and the water [newt]; that in the fury of his heart, when the foul fiend rages, eats cow-dung for sallets; swallows the old rat and the ditch-dog; drinks the green mantle of the standing pool; ...

There are, again, dire and dreadful things about toads in the rarer plays. Thus Ajax in *Troilus and Cressida* (II, iii, 158) declares: 'I do hate a proud man, as I hate the engendering of **toads**.' And the fiend-like Tamora in *Titus Andronicus* (II, iii, 101) tells how she was left in an evil spot in the forest, where

Ten thousand swelling **toads**, as many urchins [= hedgehogs], Would make such fearful and confused cries, As any mortal body hearing it Should straight fall mad, or else die suddenly.

But yet we need go no further than *Othello* – Olivier's superb in recent memory – to note the Moor's most sinister emphases in two scenes, both with Desdemona, where he mentions 'a cistern for foul **toads** to knot and gender in'

(*Othello*, IV, ii, 61), and where with infinite yearning he breathes the words (III, iii, 270):

> . . . I had rather be a **toad,**
> And live upon the vapour of a dungeon,
> Than keep a corner in the thing I love
> For others' uses.

See also under HEDGEHOG AND PADDOCK.

GARGANTUA AND GORGON

The sole reference to Rabelais in Shakespeare – the possessive form of the name 'Gargantua' – is no proof that the poet had read the great French scholar-buffoon who died eleven years before his own birth.

The reference is in *As You Like It* (III, ii, 221) when Celia tells Rosalind that she has encountered no less a man than Orlando in the forest:

ROSALIND: Orlando?
CELIA: Orlando.
ROSALIND: Alas the day! what shall I do with my doublet and hose? What did he when thou saw'st him? What said he? How lookt he? Wherein went he? What makes he here? Did he ask for me? Where remains he? How parted he with thee? and when shalt thou see him again? Answer me in one word.

This is the excitement of one 'many fathom deep in love', as she describes herself elsewhere. And Celia has her good Rabelaisian answer: 'You must borrow me **Gargantua's** mouth first: 'tis a word too great for any mouth of this age's size. . . .'

Those monster-sisters of Greek mythology, the Gorgons, have two fleeting mentions. Cleopatra says of Antony, when

[69]

she hears of his marriage to Octavia (*Antony and Cleopatra*, II, v, 116):

> Though he be painted one way like a **Gorgon**,
> The other way's a Mars.

And Macduff, having found King Duncan murdered, urges the others to go and see for themselves (*Macbeth*, II, iii, 73):

> Approach the chamber, and destroy your sight
> With a new **Gorgon**: do not bid me speak;
> See, and then speak yourselves.

Medusa, the best-known of these sight-destroying Gorgons, gets no mention at all in Shakespeare.

GEESE AND WILD GEESE

What is, or was, a Winchester Goose? It is mentioned in *King Henry VI, Part One*, where Gloster, the King's uncle, and Henry Beaufort, both a Bishop and a Cardinal, are having a public brawl before the Tower of London. Gloster calls Beaufort such things as 'peel'd [=bald] priest', 'manifest conspirator' and 'scarlet hypocrite', but the crowning insult is when he calls him 'Winchester goose' (I, iii, 53). In their efforts to explain this all the editors, like sheep, go back to a Victorian scholar, the Rev. Alexander Dyce, who died 100 years ago and who opined that the term was venereal and referred to a 'certain stage' in syphilis. It would seem that the Bishop of Winchester was in control also of Southwark, where were the worst stews in London.

So far, so bad. But Winchester Goose is mentioned also in, of all unlikely places, the last few lines of *Troilus and Cressida*. Usually, in the theatre, this play ends with Troilus rounding on and dismissing Pandarus. But in the text – and indeed in the First Folio – Pandarus has a concluding soliloquy about which nothing is very clear except its gracelessness (v, x, 45):

> Good traders in the flesh, set this in your painted cloths:
> As many as be here of Pander's hall,
> Your eyes, half out, weep out at Pandar's fall;
> Or if you cannot weep, yet give some groans,
> Though not for me, yet for your aching bones.
> Brethren and sisters of the hold-door trade,
> Some two months hence my will shall here be made:
> It should be now, but that my fear is this,
> Some gallèd **goose** of Winchester would hiss:
> Till then I'll sweat, and seek about for eases;
> And at that time bequeath you my diseases.

This probably is not Shakespeare. But whoever the writer may be, what is this debased mention of Winchester doing in ancient Troy?

There are some picturesque images of the wild goose. In *King Henry IV, Part One* (II, iv, 138) Falstaff declares to Prince Hal: 'A king's son! If I do not beat thee out of thy kingdom with a dagger of lath, and drive all thy subjects afore thee like a flock of **wild-geese**, I'll never wear hair on my face more. You Prince of Wales!' And the Fool says to King Lear when on the very verge of his madness (*King Lear*, II, iv, 46): 'Winter's not gone yet, if the **wild-geese** fly that way.'

GOATS

Goats are goatish, as men can be. And Audrey, whom Touchstone was eventually to take in marriage, was – as is not usually remembered – a goatherdess as distinct from a shepherdess.

The first of these facts is expressed by Edmund, Gloster's bastard son, in *King Lear* (I, ii, 130): 'An admirable evasion of whoremaster man, to lay his **goatish** disposition to the charge of a star!'

The second is told us, twice over, by Touchstone himself in the heart of *As You Like It* (III, iii, 1):

TOUCHSTONE: Come apace, good Audrey: I will fetch up your **goats**, Audrey. And how, Audrey? am I the man yet? doth my simple feature content you?

AUDREY: Your features! Lord warrant us! what features?

TOUCHSTONE: I am here with thee and thy **goats,** as the most capricious poet, honest Ovid, was among the Goths.

JAQUES (*aside*): O knowledge ill-inhabited, worse than Jove in a thatch'd house!

GRIFFIN AND GOBLIN

The Griffin is a fabulous animal with the head and wings of an eagle and the body and hindquarters of a lion. It seems somehow very right and proper that this rather endearing monster should be the symbol of Wales, just as the rampant red lion – shaped not at all unlike Caledonia itself – should be the standard of Scotland.

Its one, somewhat involved, appearance in Shakespeare is in *A Midsummer Night's Dream*, in Helena's speech as she pursues Demetrius, who no longer wants her (II, i, 231):

> Apollo flies, and Daphne holds the chase;
> The dove pursues the **griffin**; the mild hind
> Makes speed to catch the tiger, bootless speed,
> When cowardice pursues, and valour flies!

The *Dictionary* sense of the word 'goblin' is 'a mischievous and ugly sprite or demon'. But the word has largely lost its original force through two centuries or so of fairy tales. In Elizabethan times it could still have a more sinister power, far

more of the genuine ghostly quality. Note well Hamlet's first
address to his father's spirit at Elsinore (I, iv, 39):

> Angels and ministers of grace defend us!
> Be thou a spirit of health or **goblin** damn'd,
> Bring with thee airs from heaven or blasts from hell,
> Be thy intents wicked or charitable,
> Thou com'st in such a questionable shape,
> That I will speak to thee: I'll call thee Hamlet,
> King, father, royal Dane: O, answer me! . . .

There is more of the childish or harmless sense of 'goblin'
in little Mamillius' bedtime story in *The Winter's Tale* (II, i,
23). His mother Hermione requests it:

MAMILLIUS: Merry or sad shall't be?
HERMIONE: As merry as you will.
MAMILLIUS: A sad tale's best for winter: I have one
  Of sprites and **goblins**.
HERMIONE: Let's have that, good sir.
  Come on, sit down: come on, and do your best
  To fright me with your sprites; you're powerful at it.
MAMILLIUS: There was a man –
HERMIONE: Nay, come, sit down; then on.
MAMILLIUS: Dwelt by a churchyard: . . .

Alas that the story, so marvellously begun, got no farther since
into the scene burst Leontes in a jealous rage.

HARES

On the subject of the Hare (or *Lepus*) Shakespeare is thoroughly
outclassed by many subsequent poets. Robert Burns can coin
the perfect phrase for this animal's sportiveness in 'amorous
whids', and can turn out the perfect Scottish word for its

swift, wide-paced gait in 'hirpling'. Keats can freeze it in winter:

> St Agnes' Eve – Ah, bitter chill it was!
> The owl, for all his feathers, was a-cold;
> The **hare** limp'd trembling through the frozen grass,
> And silent was the flock in woolly fold. . . .

Wordsworth can follow it around on a spring morning (in the lovely poem about the old leech-gatherer on the moor):

> All things that love the sun are out of doors;
> The sky rejoices in the morning's birth;
> The grass is bright with rain-drops; – on the moors
> The **hare** is running races in her mirth;
> And with her feet she from the plashy earth
> Raises a mist; that, glittering in the sun,
> Runs with her all the way, wherever she doth run.

Against such delights Shakespeare can offer only some commonplace similes about the beast's cowardice and timidity, and Mercutio's abominable humour at its punning worst (*Romeo and Juliet*, ii, iii, 141):

> An old **hare** hoar,
> And an old **hare** hoar,
> Is very good meat in Lent:
> But a **hare** that is hoar
> Is too much for a score,
> When it hoars ere it be spent.

Well may Juliet's Nurse say 'Scurvy knave!' twice over, when Mercutio has marched out singing this stuff. In the mind's ear, I can still hear Edith Evans's matchless old Nurse uttering the words in crackling fury. Scurvy knave!

HARPY AND HARPIER

There is something about the Harpy repellent above all other mythological or supernatural monsters. It may be the element of filth, which the *Oxford Dictionary* emphasizes: 'a fabled monster, rapacious and filthy, having a woman's face and body and a bird's wings and claws'.

There is also a Harpy-Bat in the East Indies, and a Harpy-Eagle, which is a South American bird of prey. Doubtless they are well-named, but they come not into Shakespeare. Benedick, of course, is merely fooling when he tells Don Pedro that he will go errands to the ends of the earth 'rather than hold three words' conference with this **harpy**', meaning Beatrice (*Much Ado About Nothing*, II, i, 260). And Prospero commends Ariel for assuming the disguise of a Harpy to make a banquet vanish before it is tasted (*The Tempest*, III, iii, 83): 'Bravely the figure of this **harpy** hast thou Perform'd, my Ariel.'

But the most alarming form of the word is Harpier, which is heard and not seen. It is a familiar of the Witches in *Macbeth* (IV, i, 3). The Brinded Cat at least mewed, the Hedge-Pig at least whined, but Harpier, simply and appallingly, cried, ''Tis time, 'tis time.' Forty lines later Macbeth says to the Witches:

> How now, you secret, black, and midnight hags!
> What is't you do?

and gets the paralysing answer, 'A deed without a name.'

Harpier, their most intense familiar, may be called a shape without a name.

HAWK AND HERNSHAW

In the Induction to *The Taming of the Shrew* a drunken tinker, Christopher Sly, is treated as though he were a noble lord who had lost his reason. Shakespeare was not yet a Pirandello; he could not sustain the joke for more than a scene or two. But the fantasy certainly has its moments till it vanishes to make way for the farce itself. Sly is offered luxuries, music, horses:

> Dost thou love hawking? thou hast **hawks** will soar
> Above the morning lark: ...

And so on, from the Induction, Scene 2 (line 43).

The Hawk is used also in a comparison made by the horse-proud Dauphin of France in *King Henry V* (III, vii, 11). This Dauphin is more lyrical about his horse than Romeo about his Juliet:

> I will not change my horse with any that treads but on four pasterns. ... When I bestride him, I soar, I am a **hawk**: he trots the air; the earth sings when he touches it; ... It is a beast for Perseus: he is pure air and fire; and the dull elements of earth and water never appear in him, but only in patient stillness while his rider mounts him: he is, indeed, a horse; and all other jades you may call beasts. ...

Hamlet in his pretended madness says to Guildenstern (*Hamlet*, II, ii, 383): 'I am but mad north-north-west: when the wind is southerly I know a **hawk** from a handsaw.' The last word is corrupt, and has raised a hubbub of conjecture, and has variously appeared as 'heron', 'hernshaw' and 'heronshaw'. It is not generally known, even to the dramatic critics, that Barry Sullivan – a sonorous Irish tragedian whom Bernard Shaw injudiciously preferred to Henry Irving – accepted 'heronshaw' when he played Hamlet. He went so far as to pronounce the word 'heron ... pshaw!' When on one occasion he brought his Hamlet to Manchester, that city's great newspaper coldly advised him to desist from this malpractice.

HEDGEHOG AND PADDOCK

They are all things of evil, witches' familiars. The fairies sing to keep them away while their Queen lies sleeping (*A Midsummer Night's Dream*, II, ii, 9):

> You spotted snakes with double tongue,
> Thorny **hedgehogs**, be not seen;
> Newts and blind-worms, do no wrong,
> Come not near our fairy queen.

Caliban in *The Tempest* (II, ii, 8) sees them among the spirits with which Prospero torments and prods him:

> For every trifle are they set upon me;
> Sometimes like apes, that mow and chatter at me,
> And after bite me; then like **hedgehogs**, which
> Lie tumbling in my barefoot way, and mount
> Their pricks at my footfall; ...

Frogs or toads in the form of 'puttock' are met with elsewhere. Warwick, amid the lords with their never-ending quarrel in *King Henry VI, Part Two*, has a picturesque phrase (III, ii, 191):

> Who finds the partridge in the **puttock's** nest,
> But may imagine how the bird was dead,
> Although the kite soar with unbloodied beak?
> Even so suspicious is this tragedy.

But it is the same reptile in yet another form, that of Paddock, that is most sinister of all. It is mentioned – hardly more than mentioned – in *Macbeth* (I, i, 9) when one of the Witches

[77]

(the various editions of the play have not settled which one) says, '**Paddock** calls – anon!'

Yet another form of the word, 'Puddock', is how the frog is generally known to this day to children all over Scotland.

See under FROGS AND TOADS.

HEN AND CHICKS

The Hen is a much less nefarious creature (much less assertive and flamboyant) than the Cock. It has not even very much emotion to display as a general rule, aside from a curious trick of indignant iteration and reiteration in the announcement of the fact that it has just laid an egg. Egg-laying, indeed, may be said to go to a hen's head. But nothing else does. The Cock can be both loud and demanding, chicks querulous and inclined to twitter unendingly, but the Hen is apt to be dumb in all of that word's meanings.

Volumnia, conversing with her son, Coriolanus, compares herself to a hen without doing herself any disservice (v, iii, 160):

> ... There's no man in the world
> More bound to's mother; yet here he lets me prate
> Like one i' the stocks. Thou hast never in thy life
> Show'd thy dear mother any courtesy;
> When she, poor **hen**, fond of no second brood,
> Has cluckt thee to the wars, and safely home,
> Loaden with honour. ...

(One admiringly recalls Sybil Thorndike in the part gazing upon her Coriolanus – it was Olivier – and priding herself upon his very pride.)

The hen clucks again in a very different sort of interchange between Katharine and Petruchio (*The Taming of the Shrew*, II, i, 222):

PETRUCHIO: O, put me in thy books!
KATHARINA: What is your crest? a coxcomb?
PETRUCHIO: A combless cock, so Kate will be my **hen.**
KATHARINA: No cock of mine; you crow too like a craven.

There is Falstaff, too – in *King Henry IV, Part One*, III, iii, 54 – saying to Mistress Quickly: 'How now, Dame Partlet the **hen**! have you inquired yet who pickt my pocket?' Can there be an indication here at last that Shakespeare knew his Chaucer – Partlet being the same as Pertelote, which is the name of the hen in the Nonnes Preestes Tale? But, alas, there can be no such indication. Pertelote is ancient pre-Chaucer French for a hen, just as Chauntecleer is ancient pre-Chaucer French for a cock.

Shakespeare's few references to chicks and chickens are mainly figurative. Prospero calls Ariel 'chick' just once, at the end of the play when about to return his servant to his natural element, the air (*The Tempest*, V, i, 317):

> . . . My Ariel, **chick,**
> That is thy charge: then to the elements
> Be free, and fare thou well! . . .

This is touching. But more than touching, indeed very moving, is what Macduff says when told that his wife and children have been slaughtered by Macbeth (*Macbeth*, IV, iii, 218):

> What, all my pretty **chickens** and their dam
> At one fell swoop?

HORSE AND FOAL

Horses provide almost too broad and wide a subject for choice.

One might be dark and terrible like King Lear: 'Darkness and devils! saddle my **horses**' (*King Lear*, I, iv, 257).

Or passionate like Cleopatra: 'O happy **horse**, to bear the weight of Antony! Do bravely, horse!' (*Antony and Cleopatra*, I, v, 21).

Or impetuous like Hotspur: 'Come, let me taste my **horse**, Who is to bear me, like a thunderbolt, . . .' (*King Henry IV, Part One*, IV, i, 119).

Or desperate like Richard III: 'Give me another **horse**, bind up my wounds' (*King Richard III*, v, iii, 178).

Or mystical and Blake-like as Macbeth with his 'Heaven's cherubin, **horsed** Upon the sightless couriers of the air' (*Macbeth*, I, vii, 22).

Or imaginative like the Prologue to *Henry V* (line 26):

> Think, when we talk of **horses**, that you see them
> Printing their proud hoofs i' th' receiving earth; . . .

Or detailed and particular like the description of the perfect steed in *Venus and Adonis* (lines 295–300):

> Round-hooft, short-jointed, fetlocks shag and long,
> Broad breast, full eye, small head, and nostril wide,
> High crest, short ears, straight legs, and passing strong,
> Thin mane, thick tail, broad buttock, tender hide:
>   Look, what a **horse** should have he did not lack,
>   Save a proud rider on so proud a back.

(Hazlitt, who thought poorly of the poems as compared with the plays, said of this stanza: 'This inventory of perfections shows great knowledge of the horse; and it is good matter-of-fact poetry.')

Alternatively one might give so many single instances of other grades of horseflesh.

For example, cite Falstaff's curious and quaint question in *King Henry IV, Part Two* (II, i, 43): 'How now! whose **mare's** dead? what's the matter?'

Or repeat Lysander's criticism of Quince's delivery of the

Prologue to the play (in *A Midsummer Night's Dream*, v, i, 119): 'He hath rid his prologue like a rough **colt**.'

Or simply, like Puck, in the same play (II, i, 46), neigh 'in likeness of a **filly foal**'.

INSECTS IN GENERAL

Such insects (of the phylum *Arthropoda*) as are not dealt with elsewhere may here be dealt with severally and in alphabetical order. Here again the examples may be said to *teem*, so that choice of each single example has been the selector's.

A NTS. The *Dictionary*, not unamusingly, defines the ant as 'a small social insect of the Hymenopterous order, celebrated for its industry; an emmet, a pismire'. It is more than once mentioned by Hotspur in *King Henry IV*, *Part One*. Talking of Owen Glendower (III, i, 146):

> I cannot choose: sometime he angers me
> With telling me of the moldwarp [or mole] and the **ant**,
> Of the dreamer Merlin and his prophecies, . . .

And, still more characteristically (I, iii, 238):

> Why, look you, I am whipt and scourged with rods,
> Nettled, and stung with **pismires**, when I hear
> Of this vile politician, Bolingbroke. . . .

CRICKETS. The cricket on the hearth is *Acheta domestica*, and it is defined as a 'saltatorial orthopterous insect', which merely means that it goes by leaps and bounds, and that its wings fold lengthwise down its body. The little Prince Mamillius in *The Winter's Tale* (II, i, 30), beginning and ending his ghost story with the single sentence, 'There was a man dwelt by a churchyard', breaks off to add the words, 'I will tell it softly – Yond **crickets** shall not hear it.' A touch of genius, if one likes.

GRASSHOPPERS. The common grasshopper (*Chorthippus brunneus*) is equally saltatorial, no less orthopterous, and just as merry. Incidentally, the *Oxford Dictionary* traces this proverbial cheerfulness of the cricket only as far back as one century – 'as cheerful and lively as a cricket, 1873'. But it can be traced at least as far back as Shakespeare himself, that is to *King Henry IV, Part One* (II, iv, 88):

PRINCE HENRY: Sirrah, Falstaff and the rest of the thieves are at the door: shall we be merry?
POINTZ: As merry as **crickets**, my lad.

Elements of both these insects come into the description of Queen Mab's coach in Mercutio's celebrated scherzo for the voice (*Romeo and Juliet*, I, iv, 59). This is a synthesis of some of the finest and smallest things observable before the discovery of the microscope:

> Her wagon-spokes made of long spinners' legs;
> The cover, of the wings of **grasshoppers**;
> The traces, of the moonshine's watery beams;
> The collars **crickets'** bones; the lash, of film . . .

That this 'scurvy knave' Mercutio should have so delicate an imagination!

HONEY BEES. The distinction and the difference between, for example, a humble bee and a bumble bee is not readily made by the merely amateur hymenopterist. But it is made possible and pleasurable by John Barton's recently published *Oxford Book of Insects* (1968), especially as the illustrations are by a brilliant team led by the felicitously named Joyce Bee.

It is, oddly enough, King Henry V's Archbishop of Canterbury who gives us the poet's most elaborate metaphor on the subject of honey bees in general (*King Henry V*, i, ii, 187):

> ... so work the **honey-bees**,
> Creatures that, by a rule in nature, teach
> The act of order to a peopled kingdom.
> They have a king, and officers of sorts:
> Where some, like magistrates, correct at home;
> Others, like merchants, venture trade abroad;
> Others, like soldiers, armed in their stings,
> Make boot upon the summer's velvet buds;
> Which pillage they with merry march bring home
> To the tent-royal of their emperor:
> Who, busied in his majesty, surveys
> The singing masons building roofs of gold;
> The civil citizens kneading-up the honey;
> The poor mechanic porters crowding in
> Their heavy burdens at his narrow gate;
> The sad-eyed justice, with his surly hum,
> Delivering o'er to executors pale
> The lazy yawning **drone**. . . .

And so on for almost as long again. Henry V, who was apparently no hymenopterist, almost before His Eminence has come to a full stop, interposes, 'Call in the messengers sent from the Dauphin.'

But equally interesting, and very much less verbose, is a parallel drawn by Lucrece between herself, Collatine her husband, and Tarquin her ravisher, the parallel being with the bees (*The Rape of Lucrece*, lines 834–840). This stanza is part of the desolated Lucrece's long monody addressed to her absent husband:

> If, Collatine, thine honour lay in me,
> From me by strong assault it is bereft.
> My honey lost, and I, a **drone-like bee**,
> Have no perfection of my summer left,

> But robb'd and ransack'd by injurious theft:
> In thy weak hive a wandering **wasp** hath crept,
> And suck'd the honey which thy chaste **bee** kept.

The bee is, of course, herself, and the wasp Tarquin the ravisher.

WASPS. The wasp, which is *Vespa vulgaris*, has little in its favour except that it infinitely prefers sweetness to putrefaction. The prettiest reference to it in Shakespeare is in *The Two Gentlemen of Verona*, the nastiest in *The Winter's Tale*. In the former comedy Julia abuses herself for having torn up Proteus's love-letter to her (I, ii, 105):

> O hateful hands, to tear such loving words!
> Injurious **wasps**, to feed on such sweet honey,
> And kill the **bees**, that yield it, with your stings!
> I'll kiss each several paper for amends.

In the much later drama of jealousy Leontes, that brain-sickly and positively Strindbergian husband, tries to assure his courtier Camillo that there is method in his madness (I, ii, 326):

> Dost think I am so muddy, so unsettled,
> To appoint myself in this vexation; sully
> The purity and whiteness of my sheets,
> Which to preserve is sleep, which being spotted
> Is goads, thorns, nettles, tails of **wasps**;
> Give scandal to the blood o' the prince my son,
> Who I do think is mine, and love as mine,
> Without ripe moving to't? Would I do this?
> Could man so blench?

None who saw John Gielgud in the play's record-making revival (in 1951) will ever forget the quality of exquisite self-torture he put into such scenes.

Talking of torture, we must quote a killing devised by

Autolycus in this same play, the more so since it introduces wasps yet again. This speech is almost invariably cut in stage performance, and quite rightly too. It is in *The Winter's Tale*, IV, iii, 793:

CLOWN: Has the old man e'er a son, sir, do you hear, an't like you, sir?

AUTOLYCUS: He has a son, who shall be flay'd alive; then, 'nointed over with honey, set on the head of a **wasps'** nest; then stand till he be three quarters and a dram dead; then recover'd again with aqua-vitae or some other hot infusion; then, raw as he is, and in the hottest day prognostication proclaims, shall he be set against a brick-wall, the sun looking with a southward eye upon him, where he is to behold him with flies blown to death. . . .

But it may be that to take this over-seriously is like taking Gilbert's Mikado over-seriously.

LAPWING

The Lapwing is a crested bird (*Vanellus cristatus*) of the plover family, and its eggs are the 'plovers' eggs' of the London markets. It is also called the Pewit from its characteristic cry (Peesie in Scotland). Shakespeare uses it in one of his most endearing similes in *Much Ado About Nothing* (III, i, 24):

> For look where Beatrice, like a **lapwing**, runs
> Close by the ground, to hear our conference.

But hardly less endearing are other references. Adriana in *The Comedy of Errors* (IV, ii, 27) says, 'Far from her nest the **lapwing** cries away.' The rake Lucio, confronting the chaste Isabella in *Measure for Measure*, is moved out of his usual levity (I, iv, 31):

> I would not – though 'tis my familiar sin
> With maids to seem the **lapwing**, and to jest,

> Tongue far from heart – play with all virgins so:
> I hold you as a thing ensky'd and sainted;
> By your renouncement, an immortal spirit;
> And to be talk'd with in sincerity,
> As with a saint.

And Horatio on Osric's exit says, 'This **lapwing** runs away with the shell on his head' (*Hamlet*, v, ii, 185).

But then, it is a gentle bird with a gentle name, and Shakespeare obviously knew it well by sight.

LARKS

He knew the Lark well likewise. But before we begin to choose from his murmuration of lovely lines and phrases on the subject, let us turn to an earlier poet's couplet on this earliest of the morning's birds. One cannot swear to it that it is Chaucer (1340–1400) or Skelton (1460–1530). But it was one or the other, and both are much earlier than Shakespeare; and without being able to find or verify, one will swear to the words if not to their spelling:

> The bisy **larke**, messager of daye,
> Salueth in hir song the morwe graye

Let the poems come before the plays. From the Sonnets (No. 29) comes:

> Haply I think on thee, – and then my state,
> Like to the **lark** at break of day arising
> From sullen earth, sings hymns at heaven's gate; . . .

And from *Venus and Adonis* (lines 853–855):

> Lo, here the gentle **lark**, weary of rest,
> From his moist cabinet mounts up on high,
> And wakes the morning, . . .

[86]

The plays are not a whit less poetical on the subject. For Juliet it was the nightingale and not the lark; and for Romeo it was the lark and not the nightingale (*Romeo and Juliet*, III, v, 2, 6–7).

In the song of spring at the end of *Love's Labour's Lost* we hear that 'merry **larks** are ploughmen's clocks'. In the song of early morning in the middle of *Cymbeline* 'the **lark** at heaven's gate sings'. In the best of Autolycus's songs in *The Winter's Tale* it is the lark 'that tirra-lirra chants'.

Troilus at dawn says to his heart-breaker (*Troilus and Cressida*, IV, ii, 8):

> O Cressida! but that the busy day,
> Waked by the **lark**, hath roused the ribald crows,
> And dreaming night will hide our joys no longer,
> I would not from thee.

And the Dauphin, in the French camp near Agincourt (*King Henry V*, III, vii, 32), wants to hear praise of his horse from morn to night, which he calls 'from the rising of the **lark** to the lodging of the lamb'.

The skylark is in Scotland the laverock, and in Latin *Alauda arvensis*.

LEOPARD AND PANTHER

Talbot in *King Henry VI, Part One*, finds himself in battle near Orleans with Joan La Pucelle, and almost literally does not know where he is (I, v, 20):

> I know not where I am, nor what I do:
> A witch by fear, not force, like Hannibal,
> Drives back our troops, and conquers as she lists:
> So bees with smoke, and doves with noisome stench,
> Are from their hives and houses driven away.
> They call'd us, for our fierceness, English dogs;
> Now, like to whelps, we crying run away.

[87]

> Hark, countrymen! either renew the fight,
> Or tear the lions out of England's coat;
> Renounce your soil, give sheep in lions' stead:
> Sheep run not half so timorous from the wolf,
> Or horse or oxen from the **leopard**,
> As you fly from your oft-subduèd slaves. . . .

It is a fine zoological mêlée, and we behold in it the Leopard.

It is seen again in *Timon of Athens* (IV, iii, 327) where, as is justly said by Apemantus, 'the commonwealth of Athens is become a forest of beasts', and Timon himself surveys it: 'If thou wert the lion, the fox would beguile thee; if thou wert the lamb, the fox would eat thee: if thou wert the fox, the lion would suspect thee, when, peradventure, thou wert accused by the ass: if thou wert the ass, thy dulness would torment thee; and still thou livedst but as a breakfast to the wolf: if thou wert the wolf, thy greediness would afflict thee, and oft thou shouldst hazard thy life for thy dinner: wert thou the unicorn, pride and wrath would confound thee, and make thine own self the conquest of thy fury: wert thou a bear, thou wouldst be kill'd by the horse: wert thou a horse, thou wouldst be seized by the **leopard**; wert thou a **leopard**, thou wert german to the lion, and the spots of thy kindred were jurors on thy life: . . .'

All the Shakespearean Panthers there are occur within the same play, *Titus Andronicus*. First Titus proposes a day's hunting to the Emperor Bassianus (I, i, 491):

> To-morrow, an it please your majesty
> To hunt the **panther** and the hart with me,
> With horn and hound we'll give your Grace *bonjour*.

The hunt duly proceeds with Marcus Andronicus saying to his same lord (II, ii, 20):

> I have dogs, my lord,
> Will rouse the proudest **panther** in the chase.

It is in the same forest that Aaron the Moor leads Titus's two sons to their doom (ii, iii, 191) in that baleful play:

> Straight will I bring you to the loathsome pit
> Where I espied the **panther** fast asleep.

Both the leopard and the panther are *Felis pardus*.

LION AND LIONESS

The only two examples of *Felis leo* that one meets in all the plays – apart from countless metaphorical and figure-of-speech and heraldic lions – are the unimpressive lioness in *As You Like It* and the not unimpressive lion in *Julius Caesar*. The first beast we giggled at even in schooldays – 'a **lioness**, with udders all drawn dry' (iv, iii, 115) – and still cannot take wholly seriously in Arden, although it nearly ate Oliver de Boys, and would have done had it not been dispatched by his ill-dealt-with younger brother, Orlando.

There is, on the other hand, a kind of potency and earnestness in the Roman lion which was one of several strange portentous things seen by Cicero in the streets of Rome, a day or so before Caesar's assassination. Cicero himself describes it (*Julius Caesar*, i, iii, 19):

> Besides – I ha' not since put up my sword, –
> Against the Capitol I met a **lion**,
> Who glared upon me, and went surly by,
> Without annoying me: . . .

For the rest we can but instance six out of many leonine images:

From *King Henry V* (iv, iii, 93) the king's own **cryptic** but arresting:

> The man that once did sell the **lion's** skin
> While the beast lived, was kill'd with hunting him.

From *Measure for Measure* (I, iii, 21) the Duke's mention to Friar Thomas of one of Vienna's unenforced laws:

> Which for this fourteen years we have let slip;
> Even like an o'ergrown **lion** in a cave,
> That goes not out to prey.

From Patroclus to Achilles in *Troilus and Cressida* with one marvellous image (III, iii, 222):

> Sweet, rouse yourself; and the weak wanton Cupid
> Shall from your neck unloose his amorous fold,
> And, like a dew-drop from the **lion's** mane,
> Be shook to air.

From Aaron the Moor in *Titus Andronicus* (IV, ii, 136), proclaiming his own valour:

> Why, so, brave lords! when we join in league,
> I am a lamb: but if you brave the Moor,
> The chafed boar, the mountain **lioness**,
> The ocean swells not so as Aaron storms.

From Bottom the Weaver in *A Midsummer Night's Dream* (III, i, 31):

> For there is not a more fearful wild-fowl than your **lion** living.

From *Antony and Cleopatra* where another Messenger is whipped and Enobarbus has an aside or two (III, xiii, 89):

ANTONY: Approach, there! Ah, you kite! Now, gods and devils!
  Authority melts from me: of late, when I cried 'Ho!'
  Like boys unto a muss [= scramble *or* scrum], kings would start forth,
  And cry 'Your will?' Have you no ears? I am
  Antony yet. Take hence this Jack and whip him.

ENOBARBUS (*aside*): 'Tis better playing with a **lion's** whelp
  Than with an old one dying.
ANTONY: Moon and stars!
  Whip him.

MACKEREL AND DOGFISH

The sole reference to Mackerel requires much annotation. It is
in *King Henry IV, Part One* (II, iv, 366) in one of Falstaff's
meaty colloquies with Prince Hal:

> Well, he [Douglas] is there too, and one Mordake, and a thousand
> blue-caps more [blue bonnets ower the Border!]: Worcester is stolen
> away to-night: thy father's beard is turn'd white with the news:
> you may buy land now as cheap as stinking **mackerel**.

This could be, quite conceivably, the origin of our unidenti-
fiable proverb to the effect that 'no man cries stinking fish'.
    The sole reference to Dogfish turns out, after severe annota-
tion, to be not fishy at all but a mere term of contempt. It is
used by Talbot against the French troops led by Joan La
Pucelle in *King Henry VI, Part One* (I, iv, 107):

> Pucelle or puzzel, dolphin or **dogfish**,
> Your hearts I'll stamp out with my horse's heels,
> And make a quagmire of your mingled brains.

M.R.Ridley's note (New Temple) is perfectly adequate:
'*Puzzel* means a drab, *dolphin* is the normal Elizabethan
spelling of Dauphin, and *dog-fish* was used as a common term
of abuse.' Henry Hudson (Windsor) goes much further back
and quotes ancient books to the effect that *puzzels*, 'especially
our puzzels of Paris,' were 'filthy queans' who 'carried nose-
gays' and needed them.

MANDRAKE AND SALAMANDER

We arrive at two of the most mysterious of the Devil's creatures or creations (for assuredly they cannot be God's). They are the Mandrake and the Salamander.

Mandrakes were said to be aphrodisiacal and were thence called love-apples. The Emperor Julian tells Callixenes in his epistles that he drank the mandrake's juice as a nightly love-potion. Mandragora one supposes to be, or to have been, the essence of mandrake. The *Oxford Dictionary* begins its definition with the slightly alarming word '*Hist.*' This turns out to be merely an abbreviation for 'in historical use'. But does this mean that the mandrake is extinct nowadays?

Another valuable reference – the Centenary Edition of Brewer's *Dictionary of Phrase and Fable* – assures us that a small dose of mandragora was held to produce vanity in one's appearance, and a large dose idiocy. One would like to know what happens after a medium dose, and how *any* kind of dose is measured. Is it true that human figures used to be cut out of a mandrake root? Or that the mandrake used to scream when it was uprooted?

Shakespeare, who is often – and often deservedly – declared to tell us about everything, does at least repeat some of these legends in most pungent form. In *King Henry IV, Part Two* (III, ii, 324) we are told by Falstaff that Justice Shallow when at Clement's Inn was 'the very genius of famine; yet lecherous as a monkey, and the whores call'd him **mandrake**'. In the same play Falstaff addresses his own Page as 'thou whoreson **mandrake**' (I, ii, 15). In *King Henry VI, Part Two* (III, ii, 310) the Duke of Suffolk, a character who can be a cataract of execration, remarks:

> Would curses kill, as doth the **mandrake's** groan,
> I would invent as bitter-searching terms,

> As curst, as harsh, and horrible to hear,
> Deliver'd strongly through my fixèd teeth,
> With full as many signs of deadly hate,
> As lean-fac'd Envy in her loathsome cave: ...

And Juliet (*Romeo and Juliet*, IV, iii, 47) is fearful of the effects her drug may have:

> So early waking, what with loathsome smells;
> And shrieks like **mandrakes'** torn out of the earth,
> That living mortals, hearing them, run mad; ...

The drug mandragora has two distinct references in lines still more striking. Cleopatra asks her tactful maid Charmian for the drug, so that she may sleep through Antony's absence (*Antony and Cleopatra*, I, v, 4):

CLEOPATRA: Give me to drink **mandragora**.
CHARMIAN: Why, madam?
CLEOPATRA: That I might sleep out this great gap of time
  My Antony is away.
CHARMIAN: You think of him too much.
CLEOPATRA: O, 'tis treason!
CHARMIAN: Madam, I trust, not so.

Cleopatra does not question the drug's potency as an opiate.

But Iago does. He has been telling us how he has been busily inflaming Othello's jealousy, when the latter enters, burning like 'the mines of sulphur' and looking red-black with rage (*Othello*, III, iii, 330):

> Look, where he comes! Not poppy, nor **mandragora**,
> Nor all the drowsy syrups of the world,
> Shall ever medicine thee to that sweet sleep
> Which thou owedst yesterday.

The Salamander is a sinister creature also. It *was* a lizard-like animal and mythological, supposed to be able to live in fire.

It *is* a lizard-like animal of the *Urodela* (newts, etc.). It has the tertiary sense of being a spirit supposed to live in fire, and only in fire. Dr Brewer tells us that Francis I of France adopted as his badge the salamander, a lizard in the midst of flames, with the legend, *Nutrisco et extinguo*. This he translates for us very roughly as 'Fire purifies good metal, but consumes rubbish.' It logically follows that the salamander is, or was, good metal, and cannot, or could not, have been rubbish.

Shakespeare takes it very much less seriously than he does the Mandrake. He has but one allusion to the Salamander: he is reminded of it by the flaming red of Bardolph's nose, whose owner is called the Knight of the Lamp, for his 'face is all bubukles, and whelks, and knobs, and flames o' fire' (*King Henry V*, iii, vi, 106). But in *King Henry IV, Part One* (iii, iii, 31) Falstaff declares to the owner of this same flaming organ, 'I never see thy face but I think upon hell fire . . . thou wert indeed, but for the light in thy face, the son of utter darkness. . . . I have maintain'd that **salamander** of yours with fire any time this two-and-thirty years.'

MERMAIDS AND NEPTUNE

King Henry IV is no actor's favourite part. Falstaff and Hotspur, Prince Hal and his adorably human hangers-on steal from him both the great plays to which he gives his name. But the King has his depth as well as his dignity (and one well remembers a Stratford-on-Avon season when that valuable actor, Harry Andrews, fulfilled him to perfection, and made him nowhere dull in spite of the character's humourlessness). He has difficult but rewarding things to say like this (*Part Two*, iii, i, 45):

> O God! that one might read the book of fate,
> And see the revolution of the times

> Make mountains level, and the continent,
> Weary of solid firmness, melt itself
> Into the sea! and, other times, to see
> The beachy girdle of the ocean
> Too wide for **Neptune's** hips; how chances mock,
> And changes fill the cup of alteration
> With divers liquors! O, if this were seen,
> The happiest youth, viewing his progress through,
> What perils past, what crosses to ensue,
> Would shut the book, and sit him down and die.

In his famous description of the royal barge, Enobarbus (Ralph Richardson was ever the actor for this superb part) has his reference to the Nereides, who were Neptune's sea-goddesses, and at least fifty in number (*Antony and Cleopatra*, II, ii, 210). We have just been hearing how Antony was being fanned by 'pretty dimpled boys, like smiling Cupids', and Agrippa interrupts with his usual witty and brief comment:

> AGRIPPA: O, rare for Antony!
> ENOBARBUS: Her gentlewomen, like the Nereides,
> So many **mermaids**, tended her i' the eyes,
> And made their bends adornings: at the helm
> A seeming **mermaid** steers: the silken tackle
> Swell with the touches of those flower-soft hands,
> That yarely frame the office. From the barge
> A strange invisible perfume hits the sense
> Of the adjacent wharfs. . . .

The effect is some great canvas that Tiepolo was never to paint.

Editor Ridley (of the New Temple edition) rightly makes light of the many difficulties raised here, and in his explanation does homage to two great scholars of past time: 'There seems no sort of reason for going beyond the straightforward meaning, accepted by the straightforward Steevens and Warburton, namely, that the gentlewomen as they moved gracefully (one might say even sinuously, as befitting mermaids) made a lovely frame for the lovelier picture.'

Elsewhere Neptune is simply synonymous with the sea, though often very strikingly as in *King Richard II* where John of Gaunt has these among his splendid last words (ii, i, 61):

> England, bound in with the triumphant sea,
> Whose rocky shore beats back the envious siege
> Of watery **Neptune**, is now bound in with shame, ...

Mermaids disport themselves in many other plays and places, and lure sailors to their doom. With gloating relish does Gloster promise to do this latter in *King Henry VI, Part Three* (iii, ii, 186), 'I'll drown more sailors than the **mermaid** shall; ...' The whole soliloquy was transferred into the opening of the film of *Richard III*, and Olivier made it one of the best things in one of the best of all his performances.

MINOTAUR AND TITAN

The Minotaur was a monstrous creature with the head of a bull and the body of a man, who expected and received human sacrifices, apparently quite indifferent whether male or female, so long as they were plentiful. Titan was the god of the Sun – alternatively supposed to be twelve giants in all, six male and six female.

Shakespeare tells us very little more about either the Minotaur or Titan (or the Titans). To the former he has only a fleeting allusion in *King Henry VI, Part One* (v, iii, 187) where Suffolk says to himself about Queen Margaret who has just left his company:

> ... Suffolk, stay;
> Thou mayst not wander in that labyrinth;

> There **Minotaurs** and ugly treasons lurk.
> Solicit Henry with her wondrous praise: ...

Titan he tends to use merely as synonymous with Sun.
Thus Friar Laurence in *Romeo and Juliet* (II, ii, 1) begins his
lovely speech in his cell:

> The gray-eyed morn smiles on the frowning night,
> Chequering the eastern clouds with streaks of light;
> And flecked darkness like a drunkard reels
> From forth day's path and **Titan's** fiery wheels: ...

It would be interesting to find out whether the Elizabethan
poet, William Drummond of Hawthornden, borrowed an
idea from this when he wrote his *Summons to Love*, which has
the lines:

> The winds all silent are,
> And Phoebus in his chair
> Ensaffroning sea and air
> Makes vanish every star:
> Night like a drunkard reels
> Beyond the hills, to shun his flaming wheels.

MONSTERS IN GENERAL

Caliban is called 'monster' by the other characters repeatedly.
Trinculo, first discovering him on the shore, has this (*The
Tempest*, II, ii, 25):

What have we here? a man or a fish? dead or alive? A fish: he
smells like a fish; a very ancient and fish-like smell; ... A strange
fish! Were I in England now, as once I was, and had but this fish
painted, not a holiday fool there but would give a piece of silver:
there would this **monster** make a man; any strange beast there makes
a man: when they will not give a doit to relieve a lame beggar, they
will lay out ten to see a dead Indian. Legg'd like a man! and his fins

like arms! Warm, o' my troth! ... this is no fish, but an islander, that hath lately suffer'd by a thunderbolt. ...

Stephano, discovering Trinculo and Caliban sheltering under the same gaberdine (II, ii, 67), says, 'This is some **monster** of the isle with four legs, who hath got, as I take it, an ague.' And a few lines later, 'Four legs and two voices, a most delicate **monster**.' And he is called many other kinds of monster – shallow, weak, credulous, perfidious, drunken, puppy-headed, most scurvy, abominable, ridiculous, howling, brave, ignorant, lost, and even Monsieur Monster.

But in the end Caliban is more man than monster, however base, degraded and witch-born. And all the best Calibans on the stage – memorably that of the veteran Robert Atkins – have this quality of a creature aching to be human.

Elsewhere the word is mostly used in the absolute sense. To the pedants in *Love's Labour's Lost* it is Ignorance, to Coriolanus it is Rabble or Multitude, to Hamlet it is Custom, to Lear it is Ingratitude, to Iago it is Jealousy, 'the green-eyed **monster**'. Othello himself, nevertheless, has reference to actual physical monsters (*Othello*, I, iii, 143), and he names certain incredible creatures which came into Elizabethan cognition with the publication in 1595 of Sir Walter Raleigh's account of his travels:

> And of the Cannibals that each other eat,
> The Anthropophagi, and men whose heads
> Do grow beneath their shoulders.

MOUSE AND MOLE

Somewhere in the works of the past masters of English prose – either in Sir Thomas Browne or Robert Burton, as one remembers – there is this marvellous sentence, 'It is as a thing of naught in a great immensity, like unto a mouse in Africa.'

Shakespeare has nothing so tremendous about the mere Mouse. His similes emphasize its minuteness and its quietness. 'Have you had quiet guard?' asks Bernardo on the battlements at Elsinore; and Francisco answers, 'Not a **mouse** stirring' (*Hamlet*, I, i, 10). Falstaff says to the 'most forcible Feeble', one of his recruits, 'Thou wilt be as valiant as the wrathful dove or most magnanimous **mouse**' (*King Henry IV, Part Two*, III, ii, 164). And Lion, explaining that he is really no Lion but only Snug the Joiner, does so to the ladies in his audience (*M.N.D.*, V, i, 212), 'You, ladies, you whose gentle hearts do fear/The smallest monstrous **mouse** that creeps on floor.'

The Mole (*Talpa europaea*) is a burrowing mammal and just as 'sleekit, cowrin', timorous' as Burns called the mouse. Caliban, approaching Prospero's cell with his two new man-gods, Trinculo and Stephano, says to them (*The Tempest*, IV, i, 194):

> Pray you, tread softly, that the blind **mole** may not
> Hear a foot fall: we now are near his cell.

Hamlet says to his father's Ghost (*Hamlet*, I, v, 162), 'Well said, old **mole**! canst work i' th' earth so fast?' And Hotspur in *King Henry IV, Part One*, says how the moldwarp or mole is just one of the boring subjects discussed by Owen Glendower (III, i, 146):

> I cannot choose: sometime he angers me
> With telling me of the **moldwarp** and the ant, . . .

This common little animal, which millions of people have never set eyes on and would not recognize if they did, is still called 'mowdiewarp' in many English dialects and 'mowdie' in some Scottish ones.

NEWT AND LIZARD

These are two further contributors to the beastly olla podrida or stew of the Weird Sisters in *Macbeth* (IV, i, 14, 17) – 'eye of **newt**, and toe of frog, . . . **lizard's** leg and howlet's wing'.

'The gilded **newt**', too, is among the odd things that Timon discovers when he is digging for gold (*Timon of Athens*, IV, iii, 182). And Queen Margaret in *King Henry VI, Part Three* (II, ii, 136) tells Richard Plantagenet that he is nothing better than

> . . . a foul mis-shapen stigmatic,
> Mark'd by the Destinies to be avoided,
> As venom toads, or **lizards'** dreadful stings.

NIGHTINGALE AND PHILOMEL

The most succinct and dispassionate account of the mysterious *Titus Andronicus* is probably that of John Masefield in his book called simply *William Shakespeare* (1954):

Written (?)   *Published* (?)   *Source of the Plot* (?)

The Fable. Tamora, Queen of the Goths, whose first-born son is sacrificed by Titus Andronicus, determines to be revenged. She succeeds in her determination. Titus and his daughter Lavinia are mutilated. Two of the Andronici, his sons, are beheaded.

Titus determines to be revenged. He bakes the heads of two of Tamora's sons in a pasty, and serves them up for her to eat. He then stabs her, after stabbing his daughter. He is himself stabbed on the instant; but his surviving son stabs his murderer. Tamora's paramour (the black Aaron) is then sentenced to be buried alive, and the survivors (about half the original cast) move off (as they say) 'to order well the State'.

This is worth close comparison with the Greek mythological

legend of Philomela who was metamorphosed into the Nightingale. The abbreviated account is that of John Lempriere:

Philomela was sister to Procne who had married Tereus, King of Thrace. Procne, ever devoted to her sister, persuaded Tereus to go to Athens and bring back Philomela. On the journey Tereus became enamoured of his sister-in-law. He offered violence to her [*i.e.* violated her], and then cut off her tongue that she might not be able to report his barbarity. He confined her also in a lonely castle. Returning to Thrace he told Procne that her sister had died on the way and that he had paid the last offices to her remains. A year had nearly passed when Procne received secret information that her sister still lived. During her captivity Philomela had described her misfortunes on a piece of tapestry she had woven and had privately conveyed to Procne. The latter hastened to deliver her, and concerted with her on the best way to punish Tereus for his brutality and perfidy. She murdered her son Itylus, who was in the sixth year of his age, and served him up as food to her husband. Tereus, in the midst of his repast, called for Itylus. Whereupon Procne told him the nature of his banquet, and threw her son's decapitated head on the table to prove it. Tereus was about to slay both sisters with his sword when he was transformed by the gods into a hoopoe, Philomela into a nightingale, and Procne into a swallow.

The circumstances and the details are very different. But yet the two legends have rape and mutilation on one side of the ghastly story and unconscious cannibalism on the other. The mutilation of Lavinia is even more severe than that of Philomela since she is deprived not only of her virginity and her tongue but also of both her hands at the wrist. (All who saw the great Peter Brook production of this strange masterpiece of cruelty must remember the piteousness of Vivien Leigh as Lavinia spelling out the legend of her woes with a staff held between her handless arms. This had something of the piercing melancholy of the song of the nightingale.)

Shakespeare could easily have read Philomela's story in

Ovid or Seneca (two poets he mentions in his plays more than
once). But it has been left to today's scholarship to point out
that the plot of *Titus Andronicus* derives directly and almost
certainly from the *Thyestes* of Seneca. Professor Peter Alexander declares this in his *Shakespeare* (1964) and gives great
credit to Professor Terence Spencer of the Shakespeare Insti-
tute at Edgbaston.

The play is very early, and seems to have been composed
not long after the poems. It is therefore not surprising to find
references to the legend of Philomela, notably in *The Rape of
Lucrece* (lines 1128–1129) where Lucrece herself says to the
nightingale:

> Come, **Philomel**, that sing'st of ravishment,
> Make thy sad grove in my dishevell'd hair: . . .

For the rest Romeo and Juliet have their love-intoxicated
argument as to whether the bird that seems to comment on
them be the lark or the nightingale. And the latter word or
bird is a pet-name for Cleopatra used by Antony at the
arrogant height of their mutual rapture (*Antony and Cleopatra*,
IV, viii, 20):

> . . . My **nightingale**,
> We have beat them to their beds. What, girl! though gray
> Do something mingle with our younger brown, yet ha' we
> A brain that nourishes our nerves, and can
> Get goal for goal of youth.

OSPREY AND OSTRICH

There is a single traceable reference to the Osprey (*Pandion
haliaetus*), and but one also to the Ostrich (*Struthio camelus*).

The first is in high praise of Coriolanus, spoken by Aufidius, general of the Volscians, to his Lieutenant (*Coriolanus*, IV, vii, 33):

> I think he'll be to Rome
> As is the **osprey** to the fish, who takes it
> By sovereignty of nature.

The second is in a threat made by the rebel Jack Cade to a Kentish gentleman, Alexander Iden, who means him no harm (*King Henry VI, Part Two*, IV, x, 27): 'Ah, villain, thou wilt betray me, and get a thousand crowns of the king by carrying my head to him! but I'll make thee eat iron like an **ostrich**, and swallow my sword like a great pin, ere thou and I part.'

OTTER, WEASEL, FERRET

'What beast! why, an **otter**. – An **otter**, Sir John! why an **otter**? – Why, she's neither fish nor flesh; a man knows not where to have her.' Falstaff and Prince Hal are discussing Mistress Quickly to her face (*King Henry IV, Part One*, III, iii, 130).

In the same play Lady Percy says to her hot-headed husband, Hotspur (II, iii, 79):

> Out, you mad-headed ape!
> A **weasel** hath not such a deal of spleen
> As you are tost with.

In *King Henry V* (I, ii, 169) Westmoreland utters a calumny on Scotland's fighting habits (especially against the English):

> For once the eagle England being in prey,
> To her unguarded nest the **weasel** Scot
> Comes sneaking, and so sucks her princely eggs;
> Playing the mouse in absence of the cat,
> To spoil and havoc more than she can eat.

In *Cymbeline* (III, iv, 160) Pisanio tells Imogen that if she is successfully to masquerade as a boy she must be

> Ready in gibes, quick-answer'd, saucy, and
> As quarrelous as the **weasel**; ...

And Jaques in *As You Like It* (II, v, 11) between the two stanzas of a song of the greenwood tree, sung by Amiens, declares, 'I can suck melancholy out of a song, as a **weasel** sucks eggs.'

And the Ferret is used, only adjectivally, in *Julius Caesar* (I, ii, 182) in a marvellously vivid allusion to Cicero during a colloquy between Brutus and Cassius:

> ... look you, Cassius,
> The angry spot doth glow on Caesar's brow,
> And all the rest look like a chidden train:
> Calpurnia's cheek is pale; and Cicero
> Looks with such **ferret** and such fiery eyes
> As we have seen him in the Capitol,
> Being crost in conference by some senator.

OWL

Though there are owls of great variety of size and colour in Britain alone, Shakespeare mentions only the (Common or Barn) Owl and the Screech Owl.

The mad Ophelia (*Hamlet*, IV, v, 41) closely follows up the maddest of all her sentences with one full of the most reasonable philosophy: 'They say the **owl** was a baker's daughter. Lord, we know what we are, but know not what we may be.'

But it is the bird's association with death and the supernatural which seems most to haunt the poet. Lady Macbeth, even while waiting for her husband to enter and say he has done the deed, hears the cry of an owl (*Macbeth*, II, ii, 2):

> Hark! Peace!
> It was the **owl** that shriekt, the fatal bellman,
> Which gives the stern'st good-night.

The 'fatal bellman', usually passed over or loosely explained as 'night watchman', is much more satisfyingly noted in the New Penguin edition: 'The owl, as the bird of death, is compared to the bellman sent to give "stern'st good-night" to condemned prisoners the night before their execution.' King Duncan is the condemned prisoner.

Before Bordeaux the French General directly addresses the English Lord Talbot in *King Henry VI, Part One* (IV, ii, 15):

> Thou ominous and fearful **owl** of death,
> Our nation's terror, and their bloody scourge! . . .

Queen Tamora thus describes the evil-stricken wood where her worst longings are glutted (*Titus Andronicus*, II, iii, 96):

> Here never shines the sun; here nothing breeds,
> Unless the nightly **owl** or fatal raven: . . .

And even Queen Titania (*A Midsummer Night's Dream*, II, ii, 5) orders some elves to keep the disturbing owl well away from her lullaby:

> . . . some, keep back
> The clamorous **owl**, that nightly hoots and wonders
> At our quaint spirits. Sing me now asleep.

The word 'clamorous' almost suggests the lingering and faltering last notes of the night bird that seems loth to end her sinister howl.

For the Screech Owl one need go no further than *King Henry VI, Part Two*, where the witch, Margery Jourdain, prepares to conjure up spirits before Bolingbroke who remarks in anticipation (I, iv, 17):

Deep night, dark night, the silent of the night,
The time of night when Troy was set on fire;
The time when **screech-owls** cry, and ban-dogs howl,
And spirits walk, and ghosts break up their graves, . . .

And later, within the same play (III, ii, 327), Suffolk adds to a long list of horrors and menaces the culminating line, 'And boding **screech-owls** make the consort full!'

OYSTER

Some few allusions to the Oyster are fleeting, and are anyhow dwarfed and minimized by the superb interchange between Cleopatra and her male attendant, Alexas, who has brought news of Antony and a gift from him (*Antony and Cleopatra*, I, v, 34):

ALEXAS: Sovereign of Egypt, hail!
CLEOPATRA: How much unlike art thou Mark Antony!
Yet, coming from him, that great medicine hath
With his tinct gilded thee.
How goes it with my brave Mark Antony?
ALEXAS: Last thing he did, dear queen,
He kist – the last of many doubled kisses –
This orient pearl: his speech sticks in my heart.
CLEOPATRA: Mine ear must pluck it thence.
ALEXAS: 'Good friend,' quoth he,
'Say, the firm Roman to great Egypt sends
This treasure of an **oyster**; at whose foot,
To mend the petty present, I will piece
Her opulent throne with kingdoms; all the east,
Say thou, shall call her mistress.' So he nodded,
And soberly did mount an arm-gaunt [arm-girt? arrogant?] steed,
Who neigh'd so high, that what I would have spoke
Was beastly dumb'd by him.

[106]

PADDOCK and PUTTOCK

See under FROGS AND TOADS, also under HEDGEHOG.

Hamlet imperiously tells the Queen that his madness is but feigned, and that she must tell her husband so (*Hamlet*, III, iv, 190):

> ... 'twere good you let him know;
> For who, that's but a queen, fair, sober, wise,
> Would from a **paddock**, from a bat, a gib [= cat],
> Such dear concernings hide!

King Cymbeline asks his daughter Imogen why she chose Posthumus for a husband and not his own grotesque stepson, Cloten, and gets the answer (*Cymbeline*, I, i, 139): 'I chose an eagle, and did avoid a **puttock**.' And the sour, bitter, and voluble Thersites in *Troilus and Cressida* tells us how he would willingly be any kind of beast rather than be the cuckold Menelaus (v, i, 59): 'To be a dog, a mule, a cat, a fitchew, a toad, a lizard, an owl, a **puttock**, or a herring without a roe, I would not care; but to be Menelaus! I would conspire against destiny ...'

PARROT and PEACOCK

Neither the Parrot (*Psittacus*) nor the Peacock (*Pavo*) can inspire Shakespeare to his most felicitous style of writing. Of the former, Alexander Pope wrote: 'A very little wit is valued in a woman, as we are pleased with a few words spoken plain by a parrot.' Of the latter, William Cowper has the phrase: 'The self-applauding bird, the peacock.' Shakespeare has nothing so happy about either bird.

Mimicry, which is the parrot's special gift, combined with

the ability to imitate human speech, gets hardly a mention from Shakespeare. He comes closest to it when, in *The Merchant of Venice* (III, v, 43), young Lorenzo, the most patient of blades, grows a trifle impatient with that particularly foolish Fool, Launcelot Gobbo, and says: 'How every fool can play upon the word! I think the best grace of wit will shortly turn into silence, and discourse grow commendable in none only but **parrots**.'

Ostentation, which is the peacock's special trait, has one especial mention in *Troilus and Cressida* (III, iii, 250) where the sneering Thersites has a scalding speech on the strutting Ajax, who is preparing for a combat with Hector. It begins: 'Why, he stalks up and down like a **peacock**, – a stride and a stand: . . .' One likes to think that this may have suggested a title to Sean O'Casey for his play about the Dublin housewife, Juno Boyle, and her vainglorious husband. Whatever the source of *Juno and the Paycock*, his early play was an inspiration like its title.

Twenty-two words of verse, almost the obscurest in the whole of *Hamlet* (III, ii, 302) conclude with the very odd word 'pajock'. Presumably this is a variant of the word 'peacock'. Presumably the stanza itself, apparently improvised by Hamlet in the excitement following the Play Scene, has an inner significance:

> For thou dost know, O Damon dear,
> > This realm dismantled was
> Of Jove himself; and now reigns here
> A very, very – **pajock**.

Presumably Horatio – with his comment, 'You might have rhymed'–is being a very elementary literary critic. Presumably Hamlet's stanza is but composed of wild and whirling words – with 'pajock' the wildest of them. Presumably Editor Hudson is being something better than naïve when he comments:

'Editors have been greatly in the dark as to the reason of the word's being used here.'

PARTRIDGE, PHEASANT, WOODCOCK

Of these three game birds, the Partridge (*Perdix cinerca*) seems to be mentioned only once, the Pheasant (*Phasianus colchicus*) also once only, and the Woodcock (*Scolopax rusticula*) nine or ten times in all.

The Partridge is already killed, and cooked, but not eaten. For it appears momentarily and allusively in a speech of raillery from Beatrice to Benedick in *Much Ado About Nothing*, when each is pretending not to recognize the other at the masked ball (II, i, 140). She says of Benedick: 'He'll but break a comparison or two on me; which, peradventure, not mark'd, or not laugh'd at, strikes him into melancholy; and then there's a **partridge** wing saved, for the fool will eat no supper that night.'

The Pheasant is also ready for eating. It comes a shade surprisingly into a conversation in *The Winter's Tale* (IV, iv, 746):

AUTOLYCUS: I am courtier cap-a-pe; and one that will either push on or pluck back thy business there: whereupon I command thee to open thy affair.
SHEPHERD: My business, sir, is to the king.
AUTOLYCUS: What advocate hast thou to him?
SHEPHERD: I know not, an't like you.
CLOWN: Advocate's the court-word for a **pheasant**: say you have none.
SHEPHERD: None, sir; I have no **pheasant**, cock nor hen.

A brace of pheasants continues to this day to be a court-word for advocate in some country circles.

'Now is the **woodcock** near the gin,' says Fabian when

Malvolio is about to pick up the letter supposed to have been written by Olivia in *Twelfth Night* (II, v, 85). 'Springes to catch **woodcocks**,' says Polonius to Ophelia about Hamlet's trickery (*Hamlet*, I, iii, 115). 'As a **woodcock** to mine own springe, Osric; I am justly kill'd with mine own treachery,' says Hamlet himself (v, ii, 305). But these are all mere figures of speech. And we welcome Dumaine in *Love's Labour's Lost* (IV, iii, 80) with his 'Four **woodcocks** in a dish', until we look into the matter and discover that that too is a figure of speech and that the four 'woodcocks' are the comedy's four heroines.

PELICAN AND GULL

The Pelican is a favourite subject for jocose limericks, being an easy word to rhyme with impunity and mild daring. But the same bird is also a symbol in Christian art, and an emblem of Christ giving his blood for others. Hence some lines by John Skelton, who comes half-way in time between Chaucer and Shakespeare, which are more poignant by far than anything thing on the same subject by the latter king of poets:

> Then sayd the pellycane,
> When my byrdis be slayne
> With my bloude I them reuyue [= revive],
> Scripture doth record
> The same dyd Our Lord,
> And rose from death to lyue.

All this mysticism arose from the same bird's practice of transferring macerated food to its young from the large bag or pouch under its bill. One has seen certain varieties of domestic pigeon – notably the pouters – feeding their young in this way from their inflated crops. But they have not been sanctified for it, as has the Pelican.

This must explain why King Lear says, ''Twas this flesh begot Those **pelican** daughters' (*King Lear*, III, iv, 75). It also goes some way towards explaining why Laertes proposes to Claudius to 'ope his arms' to the friends of the dead Polonius (*Hamlet*, IV, v, 145):

> And, like the kind life-rendering **pelican**,
> Repast them with my blood.

though Laertes usually gets cut here by the director for saying anything so odd. So, usually, does the dying John of Gaunt for saying to Richard II (*King Richard II*, II, i, 126):

> That blood already, like the **pelican**,
> Hast thou tapt out, and drunkenly caroused: . . .

The word Gull in Shakespeare is used, usually, in the sense of a knave or a fool. But the web-footed bird of the same name (*Larus canus*) is obviously meant by the Earl of Worcester in his elaborate speech to King Henry (*King Henry IV*, *Part One*, V, i, 59) which goes on and on like this:

> And, being fed by us, you used us so
> As that ungentle **gull**, the cuckoo's bird,
> Useth the sparrow, did oppress our nest;
> Grew by our feeding to so great a bulk,
> That even our love durst not come near your sight . . .

We may be tempted here to interrupt with a line of Pope, 'And ten low words oft creep in one dull line'!

And there is a similar sort of mixed-up ornithology in *Timon of Athens* (II, i, 27) at the point where a Senator is telling Caphis, a creditor's servant, how to proffer his master's bill:

> Get you gone:
> Put on a most importunate aspect,
> A visage of demand; for, I do fear,
> When every feather sticks in his own wing,

[111]

Lord Timon will be left a naked **gull,**
Which flashes now a phœnix. Get you gone.

The remainder of the little scene is not perhaps Shakespeare at
his very best:

> CAPHIS: I go, sir.
> SENATOR: Take the bonds along with you,
>   And have the dates incompt.
> CAPHIS: I will, sir.
> SENATOR: Go.   [*Exeunt*

PHŒNIX

The obscurest and wildest of wildfowl is the Phœnix, almost
wholly mythical but Egyptian in origin. It is said to appear in
Egypt every 500 years, though the intervals greatly vary in
different accounts. It is said also to set itself on fire but to be
re-born in the flames. But even this characteristic has various
differing versions. It is said to have resembled the plover, but
it is also said to have resembled that very different bird, the
eagle.

The Phœnix is one of the two avian characters in Shakespeare's most unintelligible poem, the other being the Turtle
Dove. Everyone who owns a one-volume Shakespeare has
read this poem, *The Phœnix and the Turtle* – at least once but
probably never again. It is gnomic and mystical – two words
by which scholars usually mean unintelligible. One looks in
vain for any explanation or interpretation of this poem in the
great Shakespearean scholars of the past. Hazlitt eschews it and
Coleridge dodges it. So one consults two of the best Shakespearean scholars who are still with us – Ivor Brown and
George Rylands. The former in his great book, *Shakespeare*,
refers to it, only in an aside, as 'the mysterious, metaphysical,

and supposedly Shakespearean poem, *The Phœnix and the Turtle*'. The latter, after praising 'the manifestations of the passions of love' in all its forms throughout Shakespeare, adds this (in his splendid essay, *Shakespeare the Poet*): 'But in *The Phœnix and the Turtle* Shakespeare celebrates love of yet another kind, selfless, sexless, "interinanimating", as Donne puts it – not the marriage of two minds but the union of two souls:

> So they loved, as love in twain
> Had the essence but in one;
> Two distincts, division none:
> Number there in love was slain.

Shakespeare's own adventure in the metaphysical style [Mr Rylands goes on] combines at once the quality of a proposition in Euclid and of a piece of music. It is pure, abstract, symbolical and complete.' But it is also unintelligible! (One surmises, to be strictly fair, that '*own* adventure' is a misprint for '*one* adventure'.)

The Phœnix is a mysterious apparition at its every mention in the plays. When in *The Tempest* the invisible Prospero conjures up a banquet for his shipwrecked visitors (III, iii, 20) we have this interchange:

ALONSO: Give us kind keepers, heavens! – What were these?
SEBASTIAN: A living drollery. Now I will believe
That there are unicorns; that in Arabia
There is one tree, the **phœnix'** throne; one **phœnix**
At this hour reigning there.

And when at the end of *King Henry VIII* the Archbishop of Canterbury utters lengthy blessings upon the babe who is to grow up into the great Queen Elizabeth, he has this passage (V, iv, 36):

> God shall be truly known; and those about her
> From her shall read the perfect ways of honour,
> And by those claim their greatness, not by blood.
> Nor shall this peace sleep with her: but as when
> The bird of wonder dies, the maiden **phœnix**,
> Her ashes new create another heir,
> As great in admiration as herself; ...

For another reference see the quotation from *Timon of Athens* under PELICAN AND GULL.

The Phœnix is also the name of a hotel in Ephesus in *The Comedy of Errors*; and of a ship mentioned in *Twelfth Night* (v, i, 59).

PIGS, HOGS AND SWINE

'Where hast thou been, sister?' asks one Witch of another in *Macbeth* (I, iii, 2), and gets the horrid answer: 'Killing **swine**.'

It is the most sinister of several references to the beast (under this collective name), just as Cordelia's is the most tender (*King Lear*, IV, vii, 38):

> ... and wast thou fain, poor father,
> To hovel thee with **swine**, and rogues forlorn,
> In short and musty straw? Alack, alack!

The hog, well qualified, is one of the terms of abuse to which Queen Margaret can lend her rasping tongue when face to face with Gloster in *King Richard III* (I, iii, 229): 'Thou elvish-markt, abortive, rooting **hog**!'

The hog is only one of the guises which Puck proposes to assume in order to chase and tease the Athenian workmen (*A Midsummer Night's Dream*, III, i, 106):

Sometime a horse I'll be, sometime a hound,
A **hog**, a headless bear, sometime a fire,
And neigh, and bark, and grunt, and roar, and burn,
Like horse, hound, **hog**, bear, fire, at every turn.

Shylock, in his own way illustrating the theory that there is no accounting for tastes, remarks (*The Merchant of Venice*, IV, i, 47): 'Some men there are love not a gaping **pig**.' Fluellen, being Welsh, pronounces the word 'big' as 'pig' and gets himself into a pretty tangle from which he is extricated by Gower who, being English, corrects him. This exchange is in *King Henry V* (IV, vii, 13):

FLUELLEN: ... What call you the town's name where Alexander the Pig was porn?
GOWER: Alexander the Great.
FLUELLEN: Why, I pray you, is not pig great? the pig, or the great, or the mighty, or the huge, or the magnanimous, are all one reckonings, save the phrase is a little variations.
GOWER: I think Alexander the Great was born in Macedon: ...

Good playing can make this funny. But strongly unfunny is the scene in *Titus Andronicus* (IV, ii, 146) where Aaron the Moor stabs his black baby's Nurse with the mocking comment: 'Weke, weke! So cries a **pig** prepared to th' spit.'

PORPENTINE

Such is the now obsolete spelling of the Porcupine ('a rodent quadruped of the genus *Hystrix*') which bristles through several of the plays.

Thus the Ghost tells Hamlet (I, v, 18) that a full account of his harrowing story would have the effect of making

Thy knotted and combined locks to part,
And each particular hair to stand an end,
Like quills upon the fretful **porpentine**: ...

The Duke of York in *King Henry VI, Part Two* (III, i, 360) tells us something of the earlier history of Jack Cade, the rebel:

> In Ireland have I seen this stubborn Cade
> Oppose himself against a troop of kerns,
> And fought so long, till that his thighs with darts
> Were almost like a sharp-quill'd **porpentine**.

Finally the word is used as a mere term of abuse by Ajax to Thersites. This is in *Troilus and Cressida* (II, i, 24) – and it may be said here that the actor Stephen Murray made the bitterest Thersites in recollection:

AJAX: The proclamation!
THERSITES: Thou art proclaim'd a fool, I think.
AJAX: Do not, **porpentine**, do not: my fingers itch.
THERSITES: I would thou didst itch from head to foot, and I had the scratching of thee; I would make thee the loathsom'st scab in Greece.

The Porpentine was also the name of the inn at Ephesus used by various characters in *The Comedy of Errors*.

QUAIL

The Quail (*Coturnix communis*) is closely allied in family to the partridge and is similarly a much-appreciated game bird at table. That arch-gastronomer and master of English, M. André Simon, recommended it wrapped in vine-leaves which had already been soaked in cognac, and then roasted and served with a gravy made of skinned and de-seeded grapes and more cognac. Such trifles, washed down with the appropriate wine, kept that great man alive and well till he was much over ninety.

Shakespeare is not in the least concerned with the quail as provender for epicures. Thersites in *Troilus and Cressida* (v, i, 50), a master of bitter scorn and misanthropy, has what appears to be a good word for Agamemnon when he begins his tirade: 'Here's Agamemnon, an honest fellow enough, and one that loves **quails**: . . .' But he then proceeds in his more usual vein of virulent abuse.

The one other reference to quails is in *Antony and Cleopatra* (II, iii, 33) where Antony, parting from his wife Octavia, and an Egyptian soothsayer, has a curious and revealing little soliloquy which reveals (1) that quails were sometimes used instead of cocks in cock-fighting sports and (2) that Antony was already wearying of the very idea of matrimony and longing for his Cleopatra:

> . . . Be it art or hap,
> He hath spoken true: the very dice obey him;
> And, in our sports, my better cunning faints
> Under his chance: if we draw lots, he speeds;
> His cocks do win the battle still of mine,
> When it is all to nought; and his **quails** ever
> Beat mine, inhoopt, at odds. I will to Egypt:
> And though I make this marriage for my peace,
> I' the East my pleasure lies.

Here, as in many another place, Shakespeare's verse is closely parallel to Plutarch's prose.

RABBITS AND CONIES

Cony is simply the old name for the Rabbit, and is still used in the Statutes and in Heraldry. But the frequent phrase 'cony-catcher' or 'cony-catching' simply means 'cheat' or 'cheating', 'deceive' or 'deceiver'. Thus Slender in *The Merry Wives of*

Windsor (I, i, 120) has no rabbits in mind when he says to Falstaff:

Marry, sir, I have matter in my head against you: and against your **cony-catching** rascals, Bardolph, Nym, and Pistol; they carried me to the tavern and made me drunk, and afterwards picked my pocket.

But Rosalind, in the guise of Ganymede, clearly has the rabbit in mind when she is thus accosted by Orlando in the Forest of Arden (*As You Like It*, III, ii, 339):

ORLANDO: Where dwell you, pretty youth? . . . Are you native of this place?
ROSALIND: As the **cony**, that you see dwell where she is kindled.

Rabbits under their own name bound or abound elsewhere, at least figuratively. The voluble page called Moth imagines his master Don Armado singing a love song (*Love's Labour's Lost*, III, i, 17) 'with your hat penthouse-like, o'er the shop of your eyes; with your arms crossed on your thin-belly doublet, like a **rabbit** on a spit; . . .'

Bardolph applies the word to the Page as a mere term of abuse in *King Henry IV, Part Two* (II, ii, 84): 'Away, you whoreson upright **rabbit**, away!'

In *The Taming of the Shrew* (IV, iv, 98) Biondello says to Lucentio: 'I knew a wench married in an afternoon as she went to the garden for parsley to stuff a **rabbit**; and so may you, sir: and so, adieu, sir.'

Rabbit is *Lepus cuniculus* and it is said to be able to breed seven times in a year.

RATS

Among major English poets only Robert Browning, in his celebrated *Pied Piper*, has successfully coped with Rats with that good humour and wit which alone can neutralize the nastiness of the subject.

Shakespeare knows all about the nastiness. Mad Tom in *King Lear* (III, iv, 136) says that he 'swallows the old **rat** and the ditch-dog', and tells us a line or two later that 'mice and **rats**, and such small deer, Have been Tom's food for seven long year'. But as usual the Witches in *Macbeth* beat all others in sheer horribleness. The First Witch will follow the sailor (whose wife has offended her) to Aleppo (I, iii, 9):

> And, like a **rat** without a tail,
> I'll do, I'll do, and I'll do.

But what will the fiend-like hag *do*? A deed without a name?

Nor is Claudio's observation to Lucio in *Measure for Measure* (I, ii, 126) exactly uplifting or jolly:

> Our natures do pursue,
> Like **rats** that ravin down their proper bane,
> A thirsty evil; and when we drink we die.

No, the Rat (*Mus decumanus*) is, so to speak, Robert Browning's pigeon. The poem was dedicated to William Charles Macready, eldest son of the great English actor of the same name. It was written in 1842 to amuse the little boy who was on a sick-bed. This dedicatee is directly addressed in the last four lines which contain the moral of the tale. The last couplet is said to rhyme abominably by children – and their parents – who have not the sense to emphasize the two words 'from' (as here). This done, they rhyme most engagingly:

> So, Willy, let me and you be wipers
> Of scores out with all men, especially pipers!
> And whether they pipe us *from* **rats** or *from* mice,
> If we've promised them aught, let us keep our promise!

RAVEN, ROOK, CHOUGH

The Raven (*Corvus corax*) is automatically enrolled among the birds of evil by Lady Macbeth on hearing that the King of Scotland is at hand (*Macbeth*, I, v, 39):

> The **raven** himself is hoarse
> That croaks the fatal entrance of Duncan
> Under my battlements.

For a blistering curse on both Prospero and Ariel (*The Tempest*, I, ii, 321) Caliban mentions his own mother, the foul witch Sycorax:

> As wicked dew as e'er my mother brush'd
> With **raven's** feather from unwholesome fen
> Drop on you both!

Thersites in *Troilus and Cressida*, himself a habitual croaker, exclaims (V, ii, 191): 'Would I could meet that rogue Diomed! I would croak like a **raven**; I would bode, I would bode.'

The Queen of the Goths in *Titus Andronicus* (II, iii, 96) says of her blighted and baleful forest:

> Here never shines the sun; here nothing breeds,
> Unless the nightly owl or fatal **raven**: . . .

Othello compares to the raven his memory of that handkerchief (IV, i, 20):

> O, it comes o'er my memory,
> As doth the **raven** o'er the infected house,
> Boding to all, . . .

and Hamlet harangues the villain in the middle of the Play Scene (III, ii, 270): 'Begin, murderer; pox, leave thy damnable

[120]

faces, and begin. Come: the croaking **raven** doth bellow for revenge.'

These are but six of three times as many ravens that croak darkly throughout the plays. The Rook (*Corvus frugilegus*) is not nearly so much in evidence, though some odd variants of its name occur in some magic places. Thus in *King Henry VI, Part Three*, the King tells Gloster, in the long speech in the course of which the latter stabs him dead, that among the many weird happenings at Gloster's birth (v, vi, 47), 'The **raven rooked** her on the chimney's top.' And Macbeth – yet again Macbeth – has his infinitely sinister (III, ii, 49):

> Light thickens; and the crow
> Makes wing to th' **rooky** wood: ...

Of references to that other member of the crow family, the Chough, one is very seldom heard in the theatre, being in a longish speech by a minor character called First French Lord who must nevertheless seem to be speaking cogently about any international conference of this present or any other century (*All's Well That Ends Well*, IV, i, 16):

> ... therefore we must every one be a man of his own fancy, not to know what we speak one to another; so we seem to know, is to know straight our purpose; **choughs'** language, gabble enough, and good enough. As for you, interpreter, you must seem very politic.

The other reference to choughs, and to rooks likewise, is in Macbeth's searing speech to his Lady at the end of the Banquet Scene when their guests – together with Banquo's Ghost – have all departed (*Macbeth*, III, iv, 122). One clearly remembers the great Macbeth of Olivier here – seen only at Stratford-on-Avon – white with weariness, vibrant-voiced with guilt:

> It will have blood; they say blood will have blood:
> Stones have been known to move, and trees to speak;

Augurs, and understood relations have
By maggot-pies and **choughs** and **rooks** brought forth
The secret'st man of blood.

SALMON AND TROUT

Iago's remark to Desdemona (*Othello*, II, i, 155) about women
in general:

> She that in wisdom never was so frail
> To change the cod's head for the **salmon's** tail.

is just one of the villain's subtleties, and all the scholars and
editors tend to be dumb about it. But it is a fact that 200 and
more years ago a baked cod's head in a gill of red wine was
esteemed a delicacy in Boston, Mass.

There are only two mentions of the trout and both are
figurative. When Maria in *Twelfth Night* throws down her
mistress's forged letter (II, v, 22) and says 'Here comes the
trout that must be caught with tickling' she is referring to
Malvolio coming down the garden-walk (and referring also,
incidentally, to a primitive form of trout-fishing practised by
paddling little boys to this day).

The mention in *Measure for Measure* (I, ii, 82) is incomparably
less innocent, Pompey being a pimp and Mistress Overdone a
bawd in Old Vienna:

MISTRESS OVERDONE: . . . What's the news with you?
POMPEY: Yonder man is carried to prison.
MISTRESS O: Well: what has he done?
POMPEY: A woman.
MISTRESS O: But what's his offence?
POMPEY: Groping for **trouts** in a peculiar river.
MISTRESS O: What, is there a maid with child by him?
POMPEY: No, but there's a woman with maid by him.

Lastly, Fluellen's delicious Welsh comment (*King Henry V*, iv, vii, 32) that there is a river in Macedon and likewise in Monmouth, 'and there is **salmons** in both' must not be omitted.

SCORPIONS

These to Shakespeare were not examples of the arachnid of the genus Scorpio – lobster-like but a bright orange-scarlet in colour, and with a bitter sting in the tail. They were, instead, bogies and bugbears, imaginary doubts and fears.

Thus in *King Henry VI, Part Two*, that mistress of anger and pelting words, Queen Margaret, tells the King amid a downpour of speech (iii, ii, 86) that she has heard a voice say unto her:

> ... 'Seek not a **scorpion's** nest,
> Nor set no footing on this unkind shore.'

In *Cymbeline* (v, v, 43) the physician Cornelius informs the king that his daughter Imogen had been secretly disliked by his infamous and poisonous queen (incidentally, a queen without a name):

> Your daughter, whom she bore in hand to love
> With such integrity, she did confess
> Was as a **scorpion** to her sight; whose life,
> But that her flight prevented it, she had
> Ta'en off by poison.

To which King Cymbeline has an apt observation followed by an absolutely unanswerable question, all in exactly eleven words: 'O most delicate fiend! Who is't can read a woman?'

Much more familiar is the single horripilant line Macbeth addresses to his Lady, even while he is arranging a double murder, 'a deed of dreadful note' involving Banquo and his young son (*Macbeth*, III, ii, 35): 'O, full of **scorpions** is my mind, dear wife!'

SEA-MONSTERS

Shakespeare's two references to a Sea-Monster – a marvellously vague phrase in itself – are respectively general and particular.

The one is instanced by King Lear just before he utters his tremendous curse on his eldest daughter, Goneril. He is full of imprecations and distractions. 'Darkness and devils!' he begins. Then we are made to realize that he is possessed with the thought of flying to his second daughter, Regan. He interrupts himself, begins statements which he leaves unfinished. 'Prepare my horses,' he orders. Then out pours his tremendous utterance (*King Lear*, I, iv, 265):

> Ingratitude, thou marble-hearted fiend,
> More hideous when thou show'st thee in a child
> Than the **sea-monster**!

The particular reference is made by Portia in *The Merchant of Venice* (III, ii, 53) just before Bassanio makes his choice of the three caskets:

> Now he goes,
> With no less presence, but with much more love,
> Than young Alcides, when he did redeem
> The virgin tribute paid by howling Troy
> To the **sea-monster**: I stand for sacrifice;
> The rest aloof are the Dardanian wives,
> With bleared visages, come forth to view
> The issue of th' exploit. Go, Hercules!
> Live thou, I live: with much, much more dismay
> I view the fight than thou that makest the fray.

The story, taken from Ovid, is that of Hesione, daughter of the Trojan king, Laomedon, who offered Hercules six beautiful horses if he would save his daughter and slay the monster. Portia, it must be said, does not make this at all clear. Neither should she have assumed that even an Elizabethan schoolboy (or one of today) would know that Alcides is just another name for Hercules.

SERPENTS AND SNAKES

The *Oxford Dictionary* confirms one in the impression that these two words mean the same thing – one of the 'limbless vertebrates constituting the reptilian order *Ophidia*' – but that by 'serpent' we mean nowadays one of the bigger and more venomous kinds of snake.

Shakespeare has plenty of time for both. There is a mention of the Serpent in each of the long poems of his youth. Venus says to her Adonis at the very outset of her siege (lines 17–18):

> Here come and sit, where never **serpent** hisses,
> And being set, I'll smother thee with kisses; . . .

and Tarquin approaching the sleeping Lucrece for his fell purpose is similarly compared (lines 362–364):

> Who sees the lurking **serpent** steps aside;
> But she, sound sleeping, fearing no such thing,
> Lies at the mercy of his mortal sting.

But the plays themselves are a positive snake-pit or serpent-warren, and one must be selective and particular. We might even concentrate on one great play alone, like *Antony and Cleopatra*, which may be said to seethe with Ophidia. Cleopatra, extolling Antony in his absence, uses such terms as these (I, v, 23):

> The demi-Atlas of this earth, the arm
> And burgonet of men. He's speaking now,
> Or murmuring, 'Where's my **serpent** of old Nile?'
> For so he calls me: now I feed myself
> With most delicious poison: . . .

In the following act Cleopatra receives a Messenger from the still-absent Antony (II, v, 36):

MESSENGER: Good madam, hear me.
CLEOPATRA: Well, go to, I will;
  But there's no goodness in thy face: if Antony
  Be free and healthful – so tart a favour
  To trumpet such good tidings! If not well,
  Thou shouldst come like a Fury crown'd with **snakes**,
  Not like a formal man.

Two minutes later the hapless Messenger feels bound to mumble the hapless words, 'He's married, madam,' and takes to his heels on the flash of Cleopatra's knife (II, v, 75):

CHARMIAN: Good madam, keep yourself within yourself:
  The man is innocent.
CLEOPATRA: Some innocents scape not the thunderbolt.
  Melt Egypt into Nile! and kindly creatures
  Turn all to **serpents**! Call the slave again,
  Though I am mad, I will not bite him: call.
CHARMIAN: He is afeard to come.
CLEOPATRA: I will not hurt him.

A minute later the miserable Messenger has to repeat himself (II, v, 88):

MESSENGER: I have done my duty.
CLEOPATRA: Is he married?
  I cannot hate thee worser than I do,
  If thou again say 'Yes'.
MESSENGER: He's married, madam.

[126]

CLEOPATRA: The gods confound thee! dost thou hold there still?
MESSENGER: Should I lie, madam?
CLEOPATRA: O, I would thou didst,
  So half my Egypt were submerged, and made
  A cistern for scalèd **snakes**! Go, get thee hence:
  Hadst thou Narcissus in thy face, to me
  Thou wouldst appear most ugly. He is married?
MESSENGER: I crave your highness' pardon.
CLEOPATRA: He is married?
MESSENGER: Take no offence that I would not offend you:
  To punish me for what you make me do
  Seems much unequal: he's married to Octavia.

This is playwriting. And it is very often, in stage production, stupidly cut.

One other great play insists upon not being overlooked in this matter of snakes and serpents. It is the one which has 'fillet of a fenny **snake**' (IV, i, 12) among the ingredients of the grisly brew in the Witches' Cauldron. It is, incidentally, a good test of anyone's knowledge of *Macbeth*, be they students or be they even actors and actresses, to say who utters this particular line, 'Look like the innocent flower, But be the **serpent** under't' (I, v, 67). Is it Macbeth to his wife, or is it Lady Macbeth to her husband?

See also ASPS, ADDERS, VIPERS.

SHARKS

The biological description of the Shark – 'a selachian fish of the sub-order *Squali* of the order *Plagiostomi*' – is, appropriately enough, rather a mouthful. One looks up 'selachian' and finds: 'Of or belonging to the genus *Selache* of sharks; the sharks and their allies.' This is just one of the ways of dictionaries, even the best of them.

The poet probes far more deeply than the lexicologist. When in *Macbeth* (IV, i, 23) we find among the Witches' ingredients the 'maw and gulf of the ravin'd salt-sea **shark**' we realize that the poet is giving in eight words what the mere word-spinner would take at least fifty words to convey: the bottomless gullet and insatiable gorge of the vicious fish itself – the stinging taste of the lashing and hissing element in which the shark lives to eat, and eats to live – and even some of the immediate alarm engendered in the human observer by the savagely disporting and blood-boltered brute.

SHEEP, OLD AND YOUNG

Here Shakespeare is in his native and pastoral element for the nonce.

In *The Tempest* we have Iris telling Ceres of her 'turfy mountains, where live nibbling **sheep**' (IV, i, 62).

In *Troilus and Cressida* (III, iii, 311) Thersites uses the word about Achilles, figuratively and with his accustomed mordancy: 'I had rather be a tick in a **sheep** than such a valiant ignorance.'

In *The Winter's Tale* (IV, iii, 787) Autolycus has the right, healthy phrase for the old Shepherd: 'An old **sheep**-whistling rogue.'

In *The Two Gentlemen of Verona*, that infelicitous play, there are still some few felicities as when Proteus and Speed, the clown, bring to a head their punning duel (I, i, 89):

PROTEUS: The **sheep** for fodder follow the shepherd, the shepherd for food follows not the **sheep**: thou for wages followest thy master, thy master for wages follows not thee: therefore thou art a **sheep**.

SPEED: Such another proof will make me cry 'baa'.

In *As You Like It* (III, ii, 73) another duel of wits brings out the best in Corin the old shepherd and the worst in Touchstone the jester:

CORIN: Sir, I am a true labourer: I earn that I eat, get that I wear; owe no man hate, envy no man's happiness; glad of other men's good, content with my harm; and the greatest of my pride is, to see my **ewes** graze and my lambs suck.

TOUCHSTONE: This is another simple sin in you; to bring the **ewes** and the **rams** together, and to offer to get your living by the copulation of cattle; to be bawd to a **bell-wether**; and to betray a **she-lamb** of a twelvemonth to a crooked-pated, old, cuckoldly **ram,** out of all reasonable match. If thou be'st not damn'd for this, the devil himself will have no shepherds; I cannot see else how thou shouldst scape.

In *The Merchant of Venice* (I, iii, 80) there is a more or less commercial interchange between Shylock and Antonio which also involves copulation (and this maddeningly means the passage's deletion from school editions of the play):

> SHYLOCK: ... the **ewes**, being rank,
>   In th' end of autumn turned to the **rams**;
>   And when the work of generation was
>   Between these woolly breeders in the act,
>   The skilful shepherd peel'd me certain wands, ...

and so forth. Antonio interrupts the Jew with a perceptive question, and gets an answer which proves Shylock to be a wit as well as a man of the world:

> ANTONIO: Was this inserted to make interest good?
>   Or is your gold and silver **ewes** and **rams**?
> SHYLOCK: I cannot tell: I make it breed as fast: ...

In *The Winter's Tale* (I, ii, 67) Polixenes describes to Hermione the boyhood he spent with her husband Leontes:

> We were as twinn'd **lambs** that did frisk i' the sun,
> And bleat the one at the other: what we changed
> Was innocence for innocence; we knew not
> The doctrine of ill-doing, no, nor dream'd
> That any did. . . .

In *Othello* (I, i, 89) we may note Iago's blunt serenade to old Brabantio, Desdemona's father:

> Even now, now, very now, an old black **ram**
> Is tupping your white **ewe**. Arise, arise . . .

And thence we may pass on, for a conclusion, to what the young poet was writing in verse before he was a playwright at all. In *The Rape of Lucrece* (lines 463–464) he permits himself a double meaning in his description of Tarquin's hand on Lucrece's bosom:

> His hand, that yet remains upon her breast, –
> Rude **ram**, to batter such an ivory wall! – . . .

and later in the same poem (lines 677–679) it is, with the nicest mixture of indignation and gusto, that he describes the immediate aftermath of the rape:

> The wolf hath seized his prey, the poor **lamb** cries;
> Till with her own white fleece her voice controll'd
> Entombs her outcry in her lips' sweet fold: . . .

In these and other such devious ways we may let

> . . . sweetest Shakespeare, Fancy's child,
> Warble his native wood-notes wild –

which, somewhat surprisingly, is what another very young poet, John Milton, wrote in *L'Allegro* barely twenty years after Shakespeare's death.

SNAILS

The common types of the true Snail belong to the genus
Helix (especially *Helix aspersa* or *hortensis*, the common or
garden snail, and *Helix pomatia*, the edible variety).

Five of the attributes of the gasteropod which Shakespeare
recognizes and illustrates are these: it is sluggish, delicate,
retiring, unhurried, unprofitable.

Here, respectively, are the plays and places – *The Comedy of
Errors* (ii, ii, 193), *Love's Labour's Lost* (iv, iii, 334), *King Lear*
(i, v, 27), *As You Like It* (ii, vii, 145) and *The Merchant of
Venice* (ii, v, 46).

And here – again respectively – are the speakers and the
utterances:

(1) LUCIANA: 'Dromio, thou drone, thou **snail**, thou slug, thou
sot!'

(2) BEROWNE: 'Love's feeling is more soft and sensible / Than are
the tender horns of cockled **snails**.'

(3) FOOL (*to Lear*): 'I can tell why a **snail** has a house. . . . Why, to
put's head in; not to give it away to his daughters, and leave
his horns without a case.'

(4) JAQUES: 'Then the whining schoolboy, with his satchel / And
shining morning face, creeping like **snail** / Unwillingly to
school.'

(5) SHYLOCK [of Launcelot]: 'The patch is kind enough; but a
huge feeder, / **Snail-slow** in profit, and he sleeps by day /
More than the wild-cat.'

Incidentally, and as a corollary, Shakespeare in one of his
early poems improved, if anything, on the image of Berowne
(No. 2 above). He is describing Venus's recoil of terror at
seeing Adonis gored by the wild boar (lines 1033–1038):

Or as the **snail**, whose tender horns being hit,
Shrinks backward in his shelly cave with pain,
And there, all smother'd up, in shade doth sit,
Long after fearing to creep forth again;
    So at his bloody view her eyes are fled
    Into the deep-dark cabins of her head.

SPARROWS, FINCHES, ROBINS

From a swarm of Sparrows and Finches and other such little daytime birds, one must be content to pick and choose only such as Shakespeare makes particularly odd or attractive.

The best-known sparrow occurs in Hamlet's grave colloquy with Horatio just before death parts them at the end of the play (v, ii, 215):

HORATIO: If your mind dislike any thing, obey it: I will forestall their repair hither, and say you are not fit.

HAMLET: Not a whit, we defy augury: there's a special providence in the fall of a **sparrow**. If it be now, 'tis not to come; if it be not to come, it will be now; if it be not now, yet it will come: the readiness is all: since no man knows aught of what he leaves, what is 't to leave betimes? Let be.

In his comment on this passage Granville Barker uses the rare word 'fatidic', meaning 'gifted with the power of prophecy'. He writes: 'Hamlet's fatidic speech definitely alarms Horatio, who makes a move as if to stop the match after all – in which he is checked by that curt, commanding "Let be".' The two words are omitted in many editions and are indeed not in the Folio. But the best Hamlet of our middle-century, Gielgud, made them both curt and commanding last time he played the part.

In a little scene in the Masque of Ceres in *The Tempest* the gods are charmingly shown to be capable of perfectly human behaviour (IV, i, 98):

> Mars's hot minion is return'd again;
> Her waspish-headed son has broke his arrows,
> Swears he will shoot no more, but play with **sparrows**,
> And be a boy right out.

But editors do not by any means always agree that the reference is to Venus and Cupid, or that it is to Paphos her birthplace that the goddess has returned.

There is a mention of a hedge-sparrow by the Fool in *King Lear* (see under CUCKOOS); and of a bunting in *All's Well That Ends Well* (II, v, 7) where the contemptuous Lafeu says to Bertram about the flamboyant Parolles, 'I took this lark for a **bunting**.'

As for finches, Thersites in *Troilus and Cressida* calls Patroclus 'Finch-egg!' which is a very mild term of abuse for Thersites; and Bottom the Weaver includes an indeterminate finch in one of his snatches of song (*A Midsummer Night's Dream*, III, i, 129):

> The **finch**, the **sparrow**, and the lark,
> The plain-song cuckoo gray, . . .

The Robin or robin-redbreast seems to have but a single mention in Shakespeare in Speed's witty list of the attributes of any true lover in *The Two Gentlemen of Verona* (II, i, 16):

> You have learn'd . . . to wreathe your arms, like a malecontent; to relish a love-song, like a **robin-redbreast**; to walk alone, like one that had the pestilence; to sigh, like a school-boy that had lost his A B C; . . .

But Shakespeare's contemporary, John Webster, makes much more magical use of the robin in the first four lines of the Dirge in *The White Devil*:

> Call for the **robin-redbreast** and the wren,
> Since o'er shady groves they hover,
> And with leaves and flowers do cover
> The friendless bodies of unburied men.

There is no more beautiful Dirge in the language – with the exception of 'Fear no more the heat o' the sun' in *Cymbeline*.

SPIDERS AND SPINNERS

A watchman Fairy before Titania's bower sings to keep Spiders and Spinners well away (*A Midsummer Night's Dream*, II, ii, 20):

> Weaving **spiders,** come not here;
> Hence, you long-legg'd **spinners,** hence!

And Mercutio, in his dazzling impromptu about Queen Mab and her chariot, tells us of 'her wagon-spokes made of long **spinners'** legs' (*Romeo and Juliet*, I, iv, 59). So much for fairies and spiders!

Leontes, King of Sicilia, in *The Winter's Tale* has ten lines which show his tortuous thought when suspecting the conduct of his wife with his old friend, Polixenes, King of Bohemia. The lines contain a quite horrendous figure of a spider in a drinking glass (II, i, 36):

> How blest am I
> In my just censure, in my true opinion!
> Alack, for lesser knowledge! how accurst
> In being so blest! There may be in the cup
> A **spider** steept, and one may drink, depart,
> And yet partake no venom; for his knowledge
> Is not infected: but if one present
> Th' abhorr'd ingredient to his eye, make known
> How he hath drunk, he cracks his gorge, his sides,
> With violent hefts: I have drunk, and seen the **spider**.

A spider in a bottle is almost as evil a thing, even when used figuratively. In *King Richard III* that arch-mistress of malediction, Queen Margaret (widow of Henry VI), tells Queen Elizabeth (wife of Edward IV) that she need waste no sympathy on Gloster (I, iii, 242):

> Poor painted queen, vain flourish of my fortune!
> Why strew'st thou sugar on that bottled **spider**,
> Whose deadly web ensnareth thee about?
> Fool, fool! thou whett'st a knife to kill thyself.
> The day will come that thou shalt wish for me,
> To help thee curse that poisonous bunch-backt toad.

The day *does* come, nearly three acts later, when Queen Elizabeth says to Queen Margaret (IV, iv, 79):

> O, thou didst prophesy the time would come
> That I should wish for thee to help me curse
> That bottled **spider**, that foul bunch-backt toad!

This Elizabeth is no one's favourite, but she here proves she has a good memory for a curse. She also has a line in this same play (I, iii, 110) which must always raise a smile in any good audience: 'Small joy have I in being England's queen!'

SQUIRREL

That unusually endearing rodent, the Squirrel (*Sciurus vulgaris*), has little to do in Shakespeare.

A very minor mystery in *The Two Gentlemen of Verona* is why the clown Launce should mention to Proteus 'the other **squirrel**' (IV, iv, 58) when his talk, before and after this, is all of dogs, i.e. of his dog Crab and the rest of doggery:

The other **squirrel** was stolen from me by the hangman boys in the market-place: and then I offer'd her [Silvia] mine own, who is a dog as big as ten of yours, and therefore the gift the greater.

The other references are faëry matters. Mercutio tells us that Queen Mab's chariot was 'an empty hazel-nut, made by the joiner **squirrel**' (*Romeo and Juliet*, I, iv, 67); and Titania makes a charming offer to Bottom, to be executed by a remarkably daring fairy (*A Midsummer Night's Dream*, IV, i, 36):

> TITANIA: I have a venturous fairy that shall seek
> The **squirrel's** hoard, and fetch thee hence new nuts.
> BOTTOM: I had rather have a handful or two of dried peas.
> But, I pray you, let none of your people stir me:
> I have an exposition of sleep come upon me.
> TITANIA: Sleep thou, and I will wind thee in my arms.
> Fairies, be gone, and be all ways away.

Ralph Richardson's sleepy Nick Bottom was memorable here as in many other places.

STARLING

The Starling (*Sturnus vulgaris*) occurs – to the best of one's researches – only in one place in Shakespeare. But this is an advantage over a considerable number of British birds which do not occur there at all. These include such poetic-sounding birds as the bittern and the heron, the magpie, the linnet, and the kingfisher. Tits and terns are no less absent.

The Starling is brought in only because of its propensity to talk almost like a raven, if not nearly so well as a parrot. This is in *King Henry IV, Part One*, where Hotspur ('whipt and scourged with rods, Nettled, and stung with pismires' – his own self-description) is talking about – so far as one can make out whom he is talking about – Bolingbroke (I, iii, 219):

> He said he would not ransom Mortimer;
> Forbad my tongue to speak of Mortimer;
> But I will find him when he lies asleep,
> And in his ear I'll holla 'Mortimer!'
> Nay,
> I'll have a **starling** shall be taught to speak
> Nothing but 'Mortimer', and give it him,
> To keep his anger still in motion.

There is nothing else whatever about this darkling bird that trembles as it sings. Nothing, for example, about its amazing gregariousness so that a whole multitude or murmuration of starlings may be seen, as if of one accord, swooping to the eaves or roofs of public buildings in big cities. It would also seem to be a bird of exceptional good taste since the public buildings – especially in Birmingham, Liverpool and London – are actual picture galleries. This is one's own not particularly avian observation.

SWALLOW AND MARTLET

King Duncan, on the morning of the very day he is murdered in his sleep, has his famous and highly agreeable greeting to the castle in which he is to meet his doom (*Macbeth*, I, vi, 1):

> This castle hath a pleasant seat; the air
> Nimbly and sweetly recommends itself
> Unto our gentle senses.

Whereupon Banquo continues in the same vein:

> This guest of summer,
> The temple-haunting **martlet**, does approve,
> By his lov'd mansionry, that the heavens' breath
> Smells wooingly here: no jutty, frieze,
> Buttress, nor coign of vantage, but this bird

[137]

> Hath made his pendent bed and procreant cradle:
> Where they most breed and haunt, I have observed
> The air is delicate.

And then enters Lady Macbeth with her fulsome welcoming phrases.

This genial conversation is of the highest dramatic value, coming as it does between a direct hatching of regicide between host and hostess and the elaborate falsity of the lady's actual welcome. And across the conversation, as it were, flies the 'temple-haunting **martlet**' or eave-loving swallow like a symbol of peace.

The *Oxford Dictionary* says of the martlet that it is the swift (*Cypselus apus*), and of the swallow (*Hirundo rustica*) that it is not quite the same thing. It says further of the swift that it is, or was, 'formerly often confused with the swallow'. Why 'formerly'? Both fly too fleetly for any but the ornithologist to detect the difference.

Perhaps the Prince of Arragon in *The Merchant of Venice* is just temporizing not very meaningfully before Portia's caskets when he says that the fond eye 'like the **martlet**, builds in the weather on the outward wall', and perhaps it may be assumed that he is too exercised to say what he means (ii, ix, 27).

Antony's friend, Scarus, has a very striking line about Cleopatra in the sea-fight (*Antony and Cleopatra*, iv, xii, 3):

> **Swallows** have built
> In Cleopatra's sails their nests: the augurers
> Say they know not, they cannot tell; look grimly,
> And dare not speak their knowledge.

just before Antony comes in to tell us all:

> All is lost;
> This foul Egyptian hath betrayed me: . . .

Richmond in *King Richard III* (v, ii, 22) approaches Bosworth
Field with the resonant lines:

> All for our vantage. Then, in God's name, march:
> True hope is swift, and flies with **swallows'** wings;
> Kings it makes gods, and meaner creatures kings.

And Perdita reminds us that the swallow is the harbinger of
summer rather than of spring in her wondrous lines in *The
Winter's Tale* (iv, iii, 118):

> Daffodils
> That come before the **swallow** dares, and take
> The winds of March with beauty; ...

SWAN AND CYGNETS

Two lovely allusions in the early poem, *The Rape of Lucrece*,
could easily be overlooked among the references in the dramas.
One is a platitude, but a very striking one (lines 1009–1012):

> The crow may bathe his coal-black wings in mire,
> And unperceived fly with the filth away;
> But if the like the snow-white **swan** desire,
> The stain upon his silver down will stay.

And Lucrece is referring to her own violated state when she
says (lines 1611–1612):

> And now this pale **swan** in her watery nest
> Begins the sad dirge of her certain ending: ...

The curious charm of the very word 'cygnet' is brought out
in all Shakespeare's allusions to the baby swan. Prince Henry
in *King John* (v, vii, 21) has a trembling and beautiful image
just before the king, his father, is carried in, poisoned and
dying, in his chair:

> I am the **cygnet** to this pale faint swan,
> Who chants a doleful hymn to his own death,
> And from the organ-pipe of frailty sings
> His soul and body to their lasting rest.

In the very first scene of *Troilus and Cressida* the shaky hero tells Pandarus of the white wonder of his Cressida's hand 'to whose soft seizure the **cygnet's** down is harsh' (I, i, 57). And at the end of *King Henry VI, Part One* (V, iii, 55) Suffolk leads in Queen Margaret as his prisoner and says:

> Thou art allotted to be ta'en by me:
> So doth the **swan** her downy **cygnets** save,
> Keeping them prisoner underneath her wings.

Emilia in *Othello* (V, ii, 245), stabbed in the back by her own husband, has an extraordinarily moving little death scene in which she echoes her dead mistress's song of 'Willow':

> What did thy song bode, lady?
> Hark, canst thou hear me? I will play the **swan**,
> And die in music: [*Singing*] 'Willow, willow, willow.'

And Celia stoutly defends her friendship to Rosalind before her own father, the usurping Duke Frederick, in *As You Like It* (I, iii, 69):

> . . . if she be a traitor,
> Why, so am I; we still have slept together,
> Rose at an instant, learn'd, play'd, eat together;
> And wheresoe'er we went, like Juno's **swans**,
> Still we went coupled and inseparable.

Who was it who first described Shakespeare himself as 'Sweet Swan of Avon'? Most people would guess – and guess rightly – that it was Ben Jonson, but few are familiar with the poem it occurs in, or where it was first printed. The occasion was the First Folio of Shakespeare's plays which appeared in

1623, just seven years after the poet's death. Ben Jonson's was perhaps the best of a prefatory sheaf of poems in the Master's praise. To say that it was the best is not very high praise, since – as so often happens on these occasions – the writers merely tried to outvie one another in laudation. Ben Jonson's poem had the title:

> *To the Memory of My Beloved, The Author,*
> *Mr William Shakespeare*
> *And what he hath left us*

and its last ten lines run thus:

> *Sweet swan of* Avon! *what a sight it were*
> *To see thee in our waters yet appeare,*
> *And make those flights upon the bankes of* Thames,
> *That so did take* Eliza, *and our* James!
> *But stay, I see thee in the* hemisphere
> *Advanc'd and made a constellation there!*
> *Shine forth, thou starre of* poets, *and with rage*
> *Or influence chide, or cheere, the drooping stage;*
> *Which, since thy flight from hence, hath mourn'd like night,*
> *And despaires day, but for thy volume's light.*

The poem, as a whole, is no better than it should have been.

THINGS AND SHAPES

Both of these words, when used in a certain way, can have an odd and somehow scaring effect of strangeness. It may be because of their lack of outline. A Shape, in this sense, has no shape at all; and a Thing, so used, can be something unimaginable.

Hamlet has scarcely opened (I, i, 21) when Horatio, referring to the reported apparition of the dead king, says to Bernardo,

'What, has this **thing** appear'd again to-night?' and gets the reply, 'I have seen nothing.' There is in Horatio's question some scorn and some scepticism, but there is also a hint of fearfulness in the very word 'thing'.

It can be the same with the very word 'shape' or 'shapes'. When in *King Henry IV*, *Part One*, that possessed Welshman, Owen Glendower, describes the circumstances of his birth to Hotspur (III, i, 12):

> . . . at my nativity
> The front of heaven was full of fiery **shapes**,
> Of burning cressets; and at my birth
> The frame and huge foundation of the earth
> Shaked like a coward.

he is heeded by Hotspur with very rational and abusive scorn. But we in the audience are awed by Glendower's 'shapes', much more so than by his burning cressets and earth tremors.

But it is not necessary to explore beyond *The Tempest* to find instances of this peculiarly subtle use of both the words. Sometimes within the same scene, e.g.

(1) Prospero describing the death of the witch Sycorax to Ariel:

PROSPERO: Then was this island –
Save for the son that she did litter here,
A freckled whelp, hag-born – not honour'd with
A human shape.
ARIEL: Yes, Caliban, her son.
PROSPERO: Dull **thing**, I say so; . . .   (I, ii, 281)

(2) Prospero ordering Ariel to disguise himself as a sea-nymph:

>   . . . invisible
> To every eyeball else. Go take this **shape**,
> And hither come in't: go; hence with diligence!
>   (I, ii, 302)

[142]

(3) Prospero to Caliban:

> I pitied thee,
> Took pains to make thee speak, taught thee each hour
> One thing or other: when thou didst not, savage,
> Know thine own meaning, but wouldst gabble like
> A **thing** most brutish, I endow'd thy purposes
> With words that made them known.

(I, ii, 353)

(4) Miranda to Prospero (on seeing Ferdinand for the first time):

> I might call him
> A **thing** divine; for nothing natural
> I ever saw so noble.

(I, ii, 418)

(5) Prospero to Miranda (on her view of Ferdinand):

> Thou think'st there are no more such **shapes** as he,
> Having seen but him and Caliban: foolish wench!
> To the most of men this is a Caliban,
> And they to him are angels.

(I, ii, 479)

But one's own favourite use of the word 'shapes' occurs later in the same play among the stage directions (III, iii, 21, 87). The play was first printed in the First Folio, seven years after his death, and some scholars think that the directions are not from Shakespeare's own hand. If this be so, the hand was worthy of the task. The directions are thus printed and spelt in the First Folio itself:

Solemne and strange Musicke: and Prosper on the top (invisible): Enter severall strange **shapes**, bringing in a Banket [so spelt]; and dance about it with gentle actions of salutations, and inviting the King, Ec. to eate, they depart. . . .

Thunder and Lightning. Enter Ariell (like a Harpey); claps his wings upon the Table, and with a quient [*sic*] device the Banquet vanishes. . . .

[143]

He [Ariel] vanishes in Thunder: then to soft Musicke. Enter the **shapes** againe, and daunce (with mockes and mowes) and carrying out the Table.

The isle is full of Shapes and Things, as well as noises.

THRUSH, THROSTLE, JAY

Portia is passably witty to Nerissa about the long list of her suitors at Belmont, and when she comes to the French lord, Monsieur Le Bon, she says he is too many men wrapped up in one (I, ii, 57):

God made him, and therefore let him pass for a man. . . . he is every man in no man; if a **throstle** sing, he falls straight a-capering; he will fence with his own shadow: if I should marry him, I should marry twenty husbands. . . .

The two other references to the song-thrush or throstle (*Turdus musicus*) are both, appropriately enough, in songs – one, unremarkable, sung by Bottom in *A Midsummer Night's Dream* (III, i, 126), the other, very remarkable indeed, sung by Autolycus in *The Winter's Tale* (IV, ii, 10). The first is a little ditty which includes 'the **throstle** with his note so true' among a carolling company which includes also the ousel or black-bird, the wren, the finch, the sparrow, the lark, and the cuckoo. But the Autolycus lyric of twenty lines beginning 'When daffodils begin to peer' is – at least as to the first four of the six stanzas – one of the great Songs of Spring.

It is only necessary to realize that 'pugging' probably means aching, and to know with certainty that 'aunts' are 'doxies' and not relatives, to appreciate that here is magic. The first of the lines quoted have true and still heart-of-the-country feeling: the second and fifth and sixth are a dawn chorus in

[144]

words; the third and fourth have a characteristic inconse-
quence; and the seventh and eighth have a sheer bucolic bliss:

> The white sheet bleaching on the hedge,
>> With hey! the sweet birds, O, how they sing!
> Doth set my pugging tooth on edge;
>> For a quart of ale is a dish for a king.

> The lark, that tirra-lirra chants,
>> With hey! with hey! the **thrush** and the **jay**,
> Are summer songs for me and my aunts,
>> While we lie tumbling in the hay.

The jay (*Garrulus glandarius*) is coupled with the thrush for no
good ornithological reason, but solely because Autolycus
couples them in the best of his songs just quoted, 'With hey!
with hey! the **thrush** and the **jay**.'

Among the other desirable delights of his desert island
Caliban offers his new men-gods, Trinculo and Stephano, is to
'show thee a **jay's** nest' (II, ii, 176). And Mistress Ford in *The
Merry Wives of Windsor* (III, iii, 35), seeing the approach of
Falstaff with an anticipative leer on his face, says, 'We'll use
this unwholesome humidity, this gross watery pumpion
[=water melon or pumpkin]; we'll teach him to know turtles
from **jays**.' Whereupon editor Ridley of the New Temple
Shakespeare very helpfully tells us that 'doves are the type of
constancy, as jays of flightiness'.

TIGERS

In such a play as *The Two Gentlemen of Verona* it is a quite
unusual flight of fancy when Proteus says apropos of Orpheus
(III, ii, 77):

> For Orpheus' lute was strung with poets' sinews,
> Whose golden touch could soften steel and stones,
> Make **tigers** tame, and huge leviathans
> Forsake unsounded deeps to dance on sands.

There are many other allusions to the tiger (*Felis tigris*) and some of the best are in some of the least familiar places. Thus Menenius says of Coriolanus (*Coriolanus*, v, iv, 28), 'There is no more mercy in him than there is milk in a male **tiger**; that shall our poor city find.' And Romeo (*Romeo and Juliet*, v, iii, 32), in a desperate speech to his servant while he is breaking into the Capulet Monument (and in some wild and whirling words which are usually cut in performance), says

> . . . hence, be gone:
> But if thou, jealous, dost return to pry
> In what I further shall intend to do,
> By heaven, I will tear thee joint by joint,
> And strew this hungry churchyard with thy limbs:
> The time and my intents are savage-wild;
> More fierce and more inexorable far
> Than empty **tigers** or the roaring sea.

Whereupon the servant Balthazar, quitting his master as though he were an empty tiger in person, summarily leaves with the parting line, 'I will be gone, sir, and not trouble you.' Balthazar, as we say today, beats it.

The Tiger is also the name of an Ephesian inn in *The Comedy of Errors*. It is likewise the name of a ship mentioned in *Twelfth Night* (v, i, 60) as being boarded on an occasion by Antonio, the sea-captain friend of Sebastian; and of another ship mentioned by the First Witch in *Macbeth* (i, iii, 7) who chased 'the master o' th' **Tiger**' in order to 'drain him dry as hay'.

TORTOISE AND TURTLE

Both are four-footed reptiles of the order *Chelonia* – the former slow-paced, land-lubberly, and inedible; the latter aquatic and providing a uniquely delicious soup with the grace of a little added sherry.

It is said of the seedy Apothecary in *Romeo and Juliet* (v, i, 42) that 'in his needy shop a **tortoise** hung'. And Prospero uses the same word figuratively in *The Tempest* (i, ii, 317) to Ariel when we might say 'slow-coach', as here, 'Come, thou **tortoise**, when?'

Wherever Shakespeare uses the word 'turtle' he means the dove; but if in his baffling poem *The Phœnix and the Turtle* he meant the reptile and not the dove, the poem could hardly mean less than it does. See under PHŒNIX.

UNICORN

The invaluable Dr Brewer tells us what we may easily have forgotten – that two Unicorns flanked the Royal Arms of Scotland before the Union of the Crowns, and that James VI of Scotland, when he went south to be James I of England, took with him one of the Unicorns. With this he supplanted the Red Dragon which, as representing Wales, had been one of the supporters of the English shield, the other being the Lion.

Dr Brewer further sends us to Edmund Spenser in whose *Faerie Queene* (Book II, Canto 5, Lines 1–2) we may read:

> Like as a Lyon, whose imperiall powre
> A prowd rebellious **Unicorne** defies . . .

and gather that the animosity which existed between the lion and unicorn (cf. the still-surviving nursery rhyme about the couple fighting 'all round the town') is allegorical to that which existed between England and Scotland.

Shakespeare has his references. In *The Tempest* (III, iii, 22) when 'severall strange Shapes' bring in a banquet and lay it before the shipwrecked noblemen, one of the latter, Sebastian, says, 'A living drollery. Now I will believe that there are **unicorns**.' Again, Timon of Athens says to Apemantus (*Timon of Athens*, IV, iii, 335), 'Wert thou the **unicorn**, pride and wrath would confound thee, and make thine own self the conquest of thy fury.' And again, Decius Brutus tells us of Julius Caesar (*Julius Caesar*, II, i, 203):

> . . . he loves to hear
> That **unicorns** may be betray'd with trees,
> And bears with glasses, elephants with holes,
> Lions with toils, and men with flatterers: . . .

But that is all. One turns eagerly to the poems, especially to *Venus and Adonis*, hoping to chase a single Unicorn. But all in vain.

VULTURE

'Let **vultures** gripe thy guts!' says Pistol in *The Merry Wives of Windsor* (I, iii, 82); and 'Let **vultures** vile seize on his lungs also!' says Pistol again in *King Henry IV, Part Two* (V, iv, 139). In both cases he is probably quoting from some forgotten gory melodrama.

'There cannot be that **vulture** in you to devour so many . . . ,' says Macduff to Malcolm, who has been declaring himself even less fit than Macbeth for kingship (*Macbeth*, IV, iii, 73). And King Lear tells his second daughter, Regan, about the monstrousness of his first daughter, Goneril (*King Lear*,

II, iv, 134), 'O Regan, she hath tied Sharp-toothed unkindness, like a **vulture**, here.' And the old king points to his heart.

Even the *Oxford Dictionary* seems to stand a little in awe of this unlovable bird. Telling us it is one of the 'large birds of prey of the order *Raptores*', it goes on to say that these 'feed almost entirely upon carrion and have the head and neck altogether or almost featherless'.

The Vulture watches us from afar in desert places. It has calculation in both its eyes. It hates us living and it loves us dead.

WHALE AND LEVIATHAN

Shakespeare seems oddly far-fetched, or momentarily out of his depth, when referring to this monstrous Cetacean by either of its English appellations. When Henry V before Harfleur refers to the leviathan he achieves only a stilted figure *King Henry V*, III, iii, 24):

> We may as bootless spend our vain command
> Upon th' enragèd soldiers in their spoil,
> As send precepts to the **leviathan**
> To come ashore.

Oberon is positively being *outré* when he tells Puck (*A Midsummer Night's Dream*, II, i, 173) to make haste in these terms:

> Fetch me this herb; and be thou here again
> Ere the **leviathan** can swim a league.

And Puck is very much more natural and felicitous in his reply, 'I'll put a girdle round about the earth in forty minutes.'

Shakespeare's himself again when, in *The Two Gentlemen of Verona* (III, ii, 80), he tells us how Orpheus with his lute could

> Make tigers tame, and huge **leviathans**
> Forsake unsounded deeps to dance on sands.

[149]

But see under TIGER.

It is 'the belching **whale**' which threatens to swallow up the babe Marina in her infant craft (*Pericles, Prince of Tyre*, III, i, 62). Again, troops fly or die in *Troilus and Cressida* (v, v, 22) like 'scalèd sculls [which may mean schools of fish] before the belching **whale**'. In *The Merry Wives of Windsor* (II, i, 63) Mistress Ford tells us of a tempest which threw a whale ashore at Windsor 'with so many tuns of oil in his belly'. But that one turned out to be merely Sir John Falstaff.

WILD BOAR

One is obliged to the late André Simon's *Concise Encyclopaedia of Gastronomy* for this concise piece of information about the Wild Boar (*Sus scrofa*): 'The wild hog of Continental Europe, southern Asia and North Africa is believed to have provided the original stock from which all races of domestic swine have been raised. In England the gastronomic reputation of the wild boar stands on its *head* which was made into a fine Brawn, and was also used as a table decoration and a tavern sign. [E.g. The Boar's Head Tavern in Eastcheap throughout *King Henry IV, Part One* and *Part Two*.] In France the Wild Boar (*Sanglier*) is still hunted in many parts of the country, and the flesh of the young (*Marcassin*) is highly esteemed as a table delicacy.'

'Eight **wild-boars** roasted whole at a breakfast, and but twelve persons there; is this true?' asks Maecenas of Enobarbus in *Antony and Cleopatra* (II, ii, 183) of entertainment in Egypt.

But most of the other references in the plays are figurative and non-gastronomical. Petruchio, coming to woo his Shrew, asks (*The Taming of the Shrew*, I, ii, 199):

> Have I not in my time heard lions roar?
> Have I not heard the sea, puf'd up with winds,
> Rage like an angry **boar** chafed with sweat?

Aaron the Moor (*Titus Andronicus*, ɪv, ii, 138) calls himself when roused to rage a 'chafed **boar**'. It is said of Alcibiades in *Timon of Athens* (v, i, 166) that 'like a **boar** too savage, [he] doth root up his country's peace'. Richmond in *King Richard III* (v, ii, 7) is referring to Gloster (whose crest the boar was) when he says:

> The wretched, bloody, and usurping **boar**,
> That spoil'd your summer fields and fruitful vines,
> Swills your warm blood like wash, and makes his trough
> In your embowell'd bosoms, this foul swine
> Lies now even in the centre of this isle,
> Near to the town of Leicester, as we learn:
> From Tamworth thither is but one day's march. . . .

These are but a few of the more striking of the wild boar's appearances in the plays.

But it is in the succulent long poem of *Venus and Adonis* that this raging beast has his happiest hunting ground. He is, in fact, that panting tale's tertiary character. There he is plain 'boar' and his wildness is taken for granted. But in the course of the poem he is variously called 'angry-chafing', 'blunt', 'foul', and 'urchin-snouted'.

WOLF

In a mountainous waste in Wales, where he is exiled with his brother and father, Arviragus in *Cymbeline* passes these random remarks (ɪɪɪ, iii, 35):

> What should we speak of
> When we are old as you? when we shall hear
> The rain and wind beat dark December, how,
> In this our pinching cave, shall we discourse
> The freezing hours away? We have seen nothing:

> We are beastly; subtle as the fox for prey;
> Like warlike as the **wolf** for what we eat:
> Our valour is to chase what flies; our cage
> We make a quire, as doth the prison'd bird,
> And sing our bondage freely.

To which old Belisarius answers: 'How you speak!' And we echo: 'Passing well!' and repeat the passage by heart to anyone who tries to argue that *Cymbeline* is an ill-written play as well as an ill-constructed one.

But the immediate point is the line about the Wolf whose wild voracity among the animals is as great as that of the vulture and the cormorant among the birds. Shakespeare notes this attribute in other places. 'If thou wert the **wolf**, thy greediness would afflict thee, and oft thou shouldst hazard thy life for thy dinner,' says Timon of Athens to Apemantus (*Timon of Athens*, IV, iii, 333). And an unnamed Gentleman in *King Lear* (III, i, 4) has a magnificent speech (which is usually cut as the Gentleman himself is) in answer to Kent's simple question: 'Where's the king?':

> Contending with the fretful elements;
> Bids the wind blow the earth into the sea,
> Or swell the curled waters 'bove the main,
> That things might change or cease; tears his white hair,
> Which the impetuous blasts, with eyeless rage,
> Catch in their fury, and make nothing of;
> Strives in his little world of man to out-scorn
> The to-and-fro-conflicting wind and rain.
> This night, wherein the cub-drawn bear would couch,
> The lion and the belly-pinched **wolf**
> Keep their fur dry, unbonneted he runs,
> And bids what *will* take *all*.

Ariel is told by Prospero of the sound he made when he was imprisoned within a cloven pine (*The Tempest*, I, ii, 287): 'Thy groans did make **wolves** howl.' The Constable of France says of the English soldiery before Agincourt that 'they will eat like **wolves**, and fight like devils' (*King Henry V*, III, vii, 149). Other allusions to the wolf are plentiful. Yet nowhere does Shakespeare so well catch the beast's utterly ruthless savagery as John Webster does in the Dirge (already quoted) where various animals and birds are summoned to cover 'the friendless bodies of unburied men', and the ten lines end with the couplet:

> But keep the **wolf** far thence, that's foe to men,
> For with his nails he'll dig them up again.

WORM AND GLOW-WORM

Allusions to the Worm (or *Lumbricus*: 'a slender, creeping, naked, limbless animal') are too numerous to be reckoned. But for its particular mention one recalls the performance of two of our major actors in some of their best parts. 'Let's talk of graves, of **worms**, and epitaphs,' said Gielgud's Richard II, almost exultant in his sorrow at his own deposition (*Richard II*, III, ii, 146). And the same actor's Hamlet put a sly and bitter humour into his explanation of what had happened to Polonius in the end: 'A certain convocation of politic **worms** are e'en at him' (*Hamlet*, IV, iii, 21).

Similarly and vividly one recalls Olivier's Mercutio very angry indeed at being stabbed and having to die: 'A plague o' both your houses! They have made **worms**'-meat of me' (*Romeo and Juliet*, III, i, 109). And, still more brilliantly, the same actor's Hotspur who died stammering over his last word which was 'worms' (*King Henry IV, Part One*, V, iv, 83):

> HOTSPUR: O, I could prophesy,
> But that the earthy and cold hand of death
> Lies on my tongue: no, Percy, thou art dust,
> And food for –   [*Dies*

[153]

PRINCE HAL: For **worms**, brave Percy: fare thee well, great heart!

On this last unforgotten and unforgettable occasion Hotspur reached the word and Prince Hal, so to speak, helped him out with it. Whether the great actor or his director first thought of this, it was enormously affecting, an inspiration.

References to the Glow-worm are few but invariably happy. Pericles himself has a charming simile (*Pericles, Prince of Tyre*, II, iii, 43): 'Like a **glow-worm** in the night, / The which hath fire in darkness, none in light.' Titania tells her fairies how to provide night-tapers (*A Midsummer Night's Dream*, III, i, 169). They must crop the waxen thighs of humble-bees 'and light them at the fiery **glow-worm's** eyes'.

Sir Hugh Evans arranging the rout in Windsor Forest at the end of *The Merry Wives of Windsor* (v, v, 79) declares: 'And twenty **glow-worms** shall our lanterns be.' And the Ghost has a marvellous way of telling Hamlet that he scents the morning air (*Hamlet*, I, v, 89):

> The **glow-worm** shows the matin to be near,
> And 'gins to pale his uneffectual fire:
> Adieu, adieu, adieu! remember me.

Incidentally, the glow-worm (*Lampyris noctiluca*) is not a worm at all, but a beetle – the only tolerable one.

WREN

The Wren (*Troglodites parvulus*) is not only the smallest of British birds, but it lays a greater number of eggs in one season than any bigger British bird. All the same, when Sir Toby Belch says of his approaching Maria (*Twelfth Night*, III, ii, 65): 'Look, where the youngest **wren** of nine comes', it is exceedingly doubtful if he is referring to the tiny bird's big egg-production. No one knows what he means exactly, and most scholars are therefore utterly silent about it. All except Scholar Hudson in the Windsor Shakespeare who comes away with the statement: 'The expression seems to have been proverbial; the wren generally laying nine or ten eggs, and the last hatched being the smallest of the brood.' Well, well!

Bottom the Weaver sings of 'the **wren** with little quill' – by which he means its musical piping (*A Midsummer Night's Dream*, III, i, 127). And King Lear in his brain-storm declares the little bird as guilty of the joy of life as any other living creature (*King Lear*, IV, vi, 113):

> The **wren** goes to't, and the small gilded fly
> Does lecher in my sight.

In another flight of fancy Gloster in *King Richard III* (I, iii, 70) goes so far as to compare the wren with the eagle:

> I cannot tell: the world is grown so bad,
> That **wrens** may prey where eagles dare not perch:
> Since every Jack became a gentleman,
> There's many a gentle person made a Jack.

But this, of course, is characteristic irony.

The true quality of the Wren is in the combination of its minuteness and its courage. Lady Macduff in *Macbeth* (IV, ii, 9) has a marvellous metaphor for this:

> . . . for the poor **wren**,
> The most diminutive of birds, will fight –
> Her young ones in her nest – against the owl.

Here one has placed the ablative-absolute clause – 'her young ones in her nest' – between dashes, deliberately. For every Lady Macduff we have ever seen or heard utters the whole sentence in a single breath. She thus makes arrant nonsense of a peculiarly beautiful image.

Still more beautiful is the plea for pity made by Imogen in *Cymbeline* (IV, ii, 302). It is a plea to the gods because Imogen has just recovered from a dead faint to find herself lying beside the headless and bleeding corpse of the rogue Cloten which is half buried in flowers:

> Good faith,
> I tremble still with fear: but if there be
> Yet left in heaven as small a drop of pity
> As a **wren's eye**, fear'd gods, a part of it!

A wren's eye!

The scene is all but unplayable in the theatre – in its bizarre mixture of the grotesque and the horrible. Here one would recommend one of the best of all theatre-books, *Ellen Terry and Bernard Shaw: a Correspondence*, for a thorough and witty discussion as to whether *Cymbeline* itself is actable or not. This discussion runs to fully thirty pages in all, and reveals how Ellen Terry's Imogen in the Lyceum revival of 1896 was obliged to cut the 'wren's eye' passage at rehearsal, and how she felt obliged to restore it on the first night and throughout the play's run. The same letters are valuable also for the way in which they communicate what must have been Ellen Terry's adorableness in the part. In her own reminiscences, *The Story of My Life* (another treasure of a theatre-book), she herself calls Imogen 'the only *inspired* performance of these later years'; and she describes the Imogen costume designed by Alma Tadema as 'one of the loveliest dresses that I ever wore'. Her photograph in that dress – with her head thrown back, a garland in her hair, and the fingers of her left hand pressed to her lips – is just about one's favourite picture of any actress in any part. Almost better than anything in *Cymbeline*, some lines from John Keats's *Ode on Melancholy* fit this picture to perfection:

> She dwells with Beauty – Beauty that must die;
> And Joy, whose hand is ever at his lips
> Bidding adieu; ...

A wren's eye! It seems right that a book which ranges in subject between whales and Caliban, between dragons and beetles and other fearful wildfowl, should conclude with a mention of one of the smallest visible things in the whole of Nature or of Shakespeare.

INDEX OF QUOTATIONS